PEARL HARBOR!

The name flashed around the world on Sunday, 7 December 1941, as radio broadcasts and then newspaper headlines described the Japanese sneak attack on U.S. naval and military installations in Hawaii. The attacking aircraft concentrated on, and did most damage to, ships of the United States Pacific Fleet in Pearl Harbor, and that became the name of the battle which threw the United States into World War II — Pearl Harbor.

The action at Pearl Harbor lasted for one hour and fifty minutes. The war which followed lasted for 1,351 days. In the many years since that tragic day, politicians, statesmen, military experts and historians have filled unnumbered books as they tried to determine exactly what happened, why it happened, and who was responsible.

Those who were at Pearl Harbor on 7 December 1941 will never forget what happened, nor will others who only remember the shock and disbelief that swept the nation that day. One immediate result was that the little-known name of an American naval base suddenly took its place in history with other names that have stood for courage and bravery — Bunker Hill, the Alamo, and Chateau Thierry. It was first a requiem, and then a battle cry, and finally a victorious chant — *Remember Pearl Harbor!*

Decades later, all that remains to remind the world of what happened at Pearl Harbor are the rusting hulks of the battleships *Arizona* and *Utah*. And, inscribed on a wall of ageless marble, the names of men who were there on 7 December 1941 and never left.

For them, especially, remember Pearl Harbor.

PEARL HARBOR ATTACK

by

ARNOLD S. LOTT, LCDR, USN (Ret.)
ROBERT F. SUMRALL, HTC, USNR

ARNOLD S. LOTT, Lieutenant Commander, U.S. Navy, retired after twenty-seven years of active duty during which time he served in sixteen different ships. The author of *A Long Line of Ships; Most Dangerous Sea;* and *Brave Ship, Brave Men;* he is senior book editor for the U.S. Naval Institute Press.

ROBERT F. SUMRALL, HTC, U.S. Naval Reserve, has an extensive background in Naval Architecture and Marine Engineering. The author of historical articles for the U.S. Naval Institute *Proceedings,* he is recognized as a leading authority on painting and camouflage. Mr. Sumrall is a Curator at the U.S. Naval Academy Museum.

Printed by Pacific Printers, Honolulu, Hawaii

Design and Drawings: Graphic design by Robert F. Sumrall; renderings, line drawings illustrating text by Alan B. Chesley.

Back Cover: Mr. Stan Jones, Artist.
Mr. Daniel Martinez, Collection.

Honolulu, Hawaii 96818 Printed in U.S.A.
No. 1 Arizona Memorial Pl.
ISBN 0-9631388-1-2

Credits

The following offices, organizations and persons furnished information and assistance in the preparation of this publication:

Public Affairs Officer, Fourteenth Naval District
Pearl Harbor Memorial Museum
Pearl Harbor Survivors Association
Office of Representative Spark Matsunaga, Washington, D.C.
Office of Naval History, Navy Department, Washington, D.C.
United States Naval Academy Museum
The U.S. National Archives, Washington, D.C.

Publications and periodicals consulted included the following:

Battle Report, Vol. 1 — Commander Walter Karig, USNR and Lieutenant Welbourn Kelly, USNR.
History of United States Naval Operations in World War II, Vol. III — Samuel Eliot Morison
Day of Infamy — Walter Lord
Most Dangerous Sea — Arnold S. Lott
U.S. Destroyer Operations in World War II — Roscoe & Freeman
U.S. Submarine Operations in World War II — Roscoe & Freeman
Closing the Open Door — James Herzog
Ships of the U.S. Navy and Their Sponsors — Somerville & Smith
I Attacked Pearl Harbor — Kazuo Sakamaki
The record of hearings of the *Joint Committee on the Investigation of the Pearl Harbor Attack*
Japanese Naval and Merchant Shipping Losses During World War II — The Joint Army-Navy Assessment Committee
United States Navy Chronology, World War II — Office of Chief of Naval Operations
Pearl Harbor — Fleet Salvage and Final Appraisal — Wallin
United States Naval Institute Proceedings: "Pearl Harbor" by Walter F. Dillingham, May 1930; "The Attack on Pearl Harbor" by Mitsuo Fuchida, September 1952; "Hawaii Operation" by Shigeru Fukudome, December 1955; and "Ford Island" by Lieutenant Commander James E. Wise, Jr., September 1964.

All photographs are Official U.S. Navy releases except for those specifically credited to other sources.
Graphics by Alan Chesley

HISTORICAL BACKGROUND

In early times, the Hawaiian name for Pearl Harbor was *wai momi*—water of the pearl—because the water there was filled with pearl oysters. From that term there came "Pearl River," and as ships eventually began using the sheltered bays for anchorage, it became natural to call it Pearl Harbor.

The first off-island visitors to the harbor were Englishmen who arrived in HMS *King George* and HMS *Queen Charlotte,* under the command of Captain Nathanial Portlock, RN, in 1786. A party went ashore there on 3 June, and an account of that visit, the first public description of *Wai Momi,* appeared in Captain Portlock's journal in 1789.

Several British ships visited in the following decades. Captain George Vancouver called there in 1792, in HMS *Discovery,* and two years later Captain John Kendrick, in *Lady Washington,* stopped in. Captain Kendrick landed some men who assisted the King of Oahu in a battle—the first military action ever recorded for Pearl Harbor.

The pearl oysters were still the most notable item of interest in the harbor. Another Englishman, Peter Corney, visited there in 1818, and on his return to England, published an account in the London Literary Gazette for 1821, which stated that there were "many divers employed here diving for pearl oysters which are found in great plenty."

In 1825 HMS *Blonde* arrived. A naturalist aboard the ship, Andrew Bloxam, was not nearly so interested in the oysters as he was in the military possibilities of the harbor: ". . . it would form a most excellent harbor as inside there is plenty of water to float the largest ship and room enough for the whole Navy of England."

Possibly, the reason that the Union Jack does not now fly over Pearl Harbor is that the next military visitor of note there was Commodore Charles Wilkes, USN, who arrived in 1840 with the U.S. Exploring Expedition, after a long cruise to the Antarctic, through the Orient, and along the Pacific coast of America. King Kamehameha III asked Wilkes to make a survey of the harbor, and the resulting chart, titled *South Side of the Iland of Oahu, Hawaiian Islands, Showing the Harbours of Honolulu and Ewa or Pearl River,* was the first technical work performed by the U.S. Navy in the harbor.

Almost fifty years passed before anything was really done about making use of the harbor. On 29 October 1887 the Hawaiian Senate ratified a treaty giving the United States the right to establish a coaling station in Pearl Harbor. The USS *Philadelphia* and later the USS *Bennington* landed parties to do survey work in the harbor, and finally, in 1900, with an appropriation of $100,000, the first dredging began. The first ship of the U.S. Navy to actually move inside the harbor was the gunboat *Petrel,* which anchored there on 11 January 1905. In 1908, following more dredging, the channel was cleared to a width of 600 feet and a minimum depth of 35 feet. On its completion, the harbor was officially opened on 14 December 1911. The celebration involved probably the biggest ribbon-cutting ceremony ever staged in Hawaii. The armored cruiser *California,* the Pacific Fleet flagship, was the first ship in, and as she steamed through the channel she broke a red, white, and blue ribbon which had been stretched all the way across the entrance, from shore to shore.

Ford Island, in the center of Pearl Harbor, was originally known as *Mokuumeume*—"island of strife." The first recorded owner was Don F. Francisco de Paula y Marin, a Spanish interpreter to King Kamehameha I. The British survey of 1825 named the place Rabbit Island. In 1865 James L. Dowsett bought the island for $1,040, and then sold it to a Miss Caroline Jackson for one dollar. The following year she married a Boston physician, Seth Porter Ford, and that name has stayed with the island ever since.

The island was transferred to the government during World War I. Its first military unit was the Army's Sixth Aero Company. The Navy first used the island in 1923. For a long time, there were two air stations on the island; the Army's Luke Field on the Pearl City side and the Naval Air Station on the other side. In 1939 Luke Field was abandoned when the Army moved to Hickam Field. The Naval Air Station was decommissioned on 31 March 1962.

The war between the United States and Japan began suddenly, but the conditions which led to war were the result of a long chain of events which commenced with Japan's aggressive move into China in 1937, and her move to assume more power in the Pacific. In subsequent months and years, these dates were significant:

26 January 1940 United States—Japanese Trade Treaty of 1911 expired.

2 April 1940 U.S. Fleet sailed from West Coast ports for maneuvers in Hawaiian area.

7 May 1940 President Roosevelt ordered the Fleet to remain in Hawaiian waters indefinitely.

5 July 1940 Roosevelt invoked the Export Control Act against Japan by prohibiting, without license, the export of strategic minerals and chemicals, aircraft engines, parts and equipment.

26 July 1940 Roosevelt invoked the Export Control Act and prohibited export, without license, of aviation gasoline and certain classes of iron and steel scrap; this halted flow to Japan.

8 October 1940 U.S. advised citizens to leave the Far East. Japan protested U.S. embargo on aviation gasoline and scrap metal.

7 July 1941 Japan recalled all merchant ships from Atlantic Ocean and called up more than 1,000,000 Army conscripts.

26 July 1941 United States froze Japanese and Chinese assets in U.S.

Pearl Harbor from the air, 31 October 1941. Ford Island is in the center with an aircraft carrier, and five battleships moored along the right side. Hickam Field air strip at far right, channel to sea at bottom center.

28 **July** 1941 Japan froze U.S. assets.

17 **August** 1941 President and Secretary of State conferred with Japanese diplomats on matter of a Pacific conference.

17 **October** 1941 U.S. Navy ordered all U.S. merchantmen in Asiatic waters to put into friendly ports.

14 **November** 1941 U.S. Marines ordered out of Shanghai, Peiping, and Tientsin, China.

20 **November** 1941 Ambassador Nomura presented Japan's "final proposal" to keep peace in the Pacific.

25 **November** 1941 Japanese troop transports sighted off Formosa, en route to Malaya.

27 **November** 1941 Chief of Naval Operations Admiral H. R. Stark sent "war warning" message to commanders of Pacific and Asiatic Fleets.

29 **November** 1941 President Roosevelt directed the Commander in Chief, Asiatic Fleet to charter three small vessels, establish their identities as U.S. men-of-war, and to station them in the West China Sea and Gulf of Siam. (If the Japanese had fired on any of these craft, it would have constituted an overt act.)

30 **November** 1941 Japanese Foreign Minister Tojo rejected U.S. proposals for settling Far Eastern crisis.

2 **December** 1941 U.S. intercepted Japanese code message directing all diplomatic and consular posts to destroy codes and ciphers, burn confidential and secret material.

PLANNING FOR HAWAII OPERATION

The attack on Hawaii was referred to by the Japanese as the "Hawaii Operation." It was no spur of the moment, "let's go hit the Americans" venture, but a carefully planned, well-thought out operation—exactly the same sort of thing which the U.S. Navy, in turn, used to sweep the Imperial Japanese Navy from the Pacific Ocean in the 44 months following Pearl Harbor.

In Japan, there had never been any question about why the country supported a navy. Since 1909, the only enemy the Japanese Navy had ever considered was the U.S. Navy. As tension grew in the Pacific, the problem was not so much who to fight as how and when to fight. The U.S. embargo

Fleet Admiral Isoroku Yamamoto, Imperial Japanese Navy, Commander in Chief of the Japanese Combined Fleet initiated plans for the attack. **IJN Photo.**

on oil only hastened the decision: Japan imported 88 per cent of her oil, and 80 per cent of that came from the United States. Without oil, the Army and Navy would be useless anywhere. A second factor was the decision, by Roosevelt, to keep the fleet in Hawaii in 1940. This Japan viewed as determination to use force in opposition to Japan's China policy. By 1940, Japan had stockpiled enough oil to last two years, but as the U.S., Great Britain, and the Netherlands had cut off the supply, the country had to get oil somewhere or face economic, and perhaps military ruin.

A new Japanese cabinet was formed in July of 1941, with Admiral Teijiro Toyoda as foreign minister, and one of Toyoda's first moves was to tell the U.S. that Japan intended to get the raw materials she needed. On 6 September 1941, it was decided that Japan would go to war with the U.S. when necessary.

Some thought had already been given to this by Admiral Isoroku Yamamoto. Late in 1940 he had discussed his ideas with Rear Admiral Shigeru Fukudome, stressing the fact that he wanted a flier to work on developing a surprise air attack, and then turned over to Rear Admiral Takajiro Ohnishi, a naval aviator, the responsibility for planning "Hawaii Operation." Early in September of 1941 Admiral Ohnishi had second thoughts about the operation; he considered it too risky and wanted to give it up. Admiral Yamamoto would not consider the proposal. On the sixth of that month, at an Imperial Conference, the decision was made to put the plan in operation.

***Vice Admiral Chuichi Nagumo, IJN, First Fleet Air Commander, led the Japanese Striking Force which launched the air attacks on Hawaii.* IJN Photo.**

***Another view of Pearl Harbor on 31 October 1941. Paired cruisers in immediate foreground, nests of destroyers to the right. White ship is the hospital ship* Solace.**

The Japanese had to consider many factors in preparing their plan. Pearl Harbor was very shallow (45 feet) and had narrow channels, making it impossible to air-drop conventional torpedoes which had to run a considerable distance in order to arm themselves. They modified the torpedoes to arm after a very short run. Commander Mitsuo Fuchida (who led the attack of 7 December) was ordered to report to the First Fleet Air Commander, Vice Admiral Chuichi Nagumo, in the aircraft carrier *Akagi* early in September, to discuss with his staff the plans for the attack. Fuchida was particularly charged with solving the problem of shallow-water launching of torpedoes; by November it was determined that adding more fins to the torpedoes would prevent them from nosing into the bottom.

The ships forming the attack group would have to assemble in complete secrecy. For this, a remote harbor in the Kuriles, Tankan Bay, was chosen, and the ships headed there over a period of several days, to avoid any appearance of mass departure from the usual Japanese ports.

Japanese fleet at Tankan Bay in the Kuriles, just before the sortie for **Hawaii Operation.**

The route to Hawaii had to avoid usual steamer lanes as much as possible, so a track across the northern Pacific and then slanting down to Hawaii from a point about 1,000 miles north was selected. The Japanese tested their selection in October by sending the merchant steamer *Taiyo Maru* across the Pacific on the route, with Lieutenant Suguru Suzuki aboard to observe wind and sea conditions. He noted that there were no ships operating in that part of the Pacific.

The Japanese knew that U.S. patrol planes searched out as far as 600 miles from Hawaii, so the final run in to launching point had to be at night, to avoid air search. With the carriers went destroyers, cruisers, and battleships, most of which did not have the cruising radius to make a 7,500 mile round trip from the Kuriles to Hawaii and return without refueling, so tankers had to go along with the force. But tankers were slower than combatant ships; this meant the force would have to refuel in time to let the tankers start home well before it began the high speed run in to the launching area.

The torpedo bombers to be used had a cruising speed of only 166 miles per hour, and a total range at that speed of about a thousand miles. Any evasive tactics, maneuvering for launching positions, or high speed operations, would greatly reduce their range. The dive-bombers had about the same capabilities; the fighters were faster but had no greater range. For this reason, the carriers had to move in fairly close to the target—200 miles—and they had to launch the aircraft in time to allow them to form up, run in to Pearl Harbor, and commence their attack just at 8 a.m. Sunrise would be at 6:26 a.m., so the planes could be launched in full dawn twilight and be on their way by sun-up.

The actual attack involved low-level torpedo bombers to hit ships in Pearl Harbor, dive bombers to knock out air fields around the island before any fighters could be scrambled to intercept the raid, high-level bombers to finish off battleships or other targets as necessary, and fighters to furnish air cover. Six carriers were assigned to the carrier task force: *Akagi, Kaga, Soryu, Hiryu, Zuikaku* and *Shokaku.* They would carry a total of 354 aircraft of all types. The cruisers and battleships screening them carried float planes for reconnaissance purposes.

Along with the air attack, extensive submarine operations were planned, with twenty-seven submarines involved. Organized as the Japanese Advance Force, they were to perform reconnaissance duties, launch underwater attacks in coordination with the air attack, sink any U.S. Navy vessels which escaped the harbor or were confused by the attack, and to intercept any reinforcements heading for Hawaii from the West Coast. Five of these submarines were to each carry a midget sub, known as "Target A," for release upon arrival off Oahu.

Track Chart for Japanese ships assigned to Hawaii Operation. *East Longitude dates west of 180°, West Longitude dates east of 180°.*

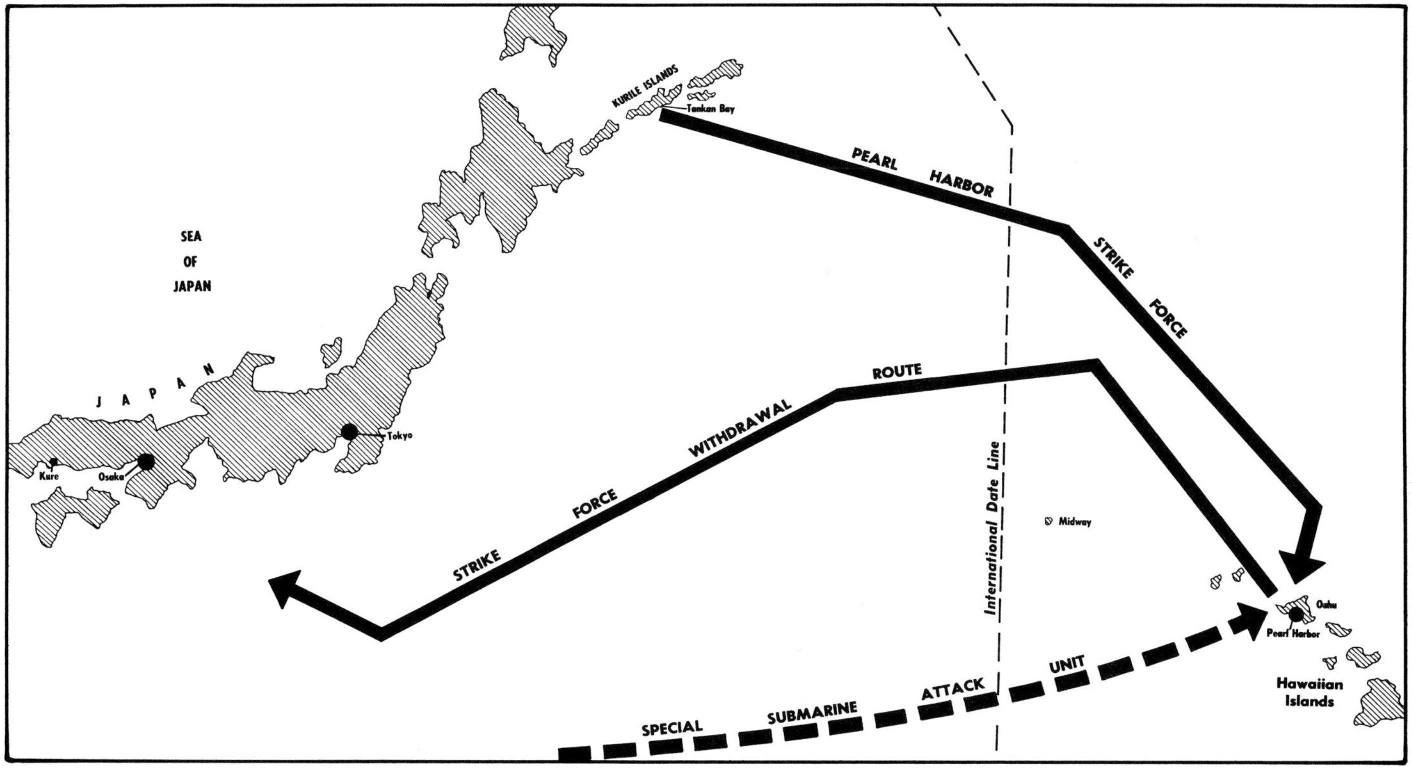

Late in August Admiral Yamamoto ordered all fleet commanders and other key staff members to Tokyo to determine the final operation plans for a Pacific campaign which would include a surprise attack on Pearl Harbor. The basic outline was completed on 13 September. When all the details of *Combined Fleet Top Secret Operation Order No. 1* had been ironed out and reduced to printed form it ran to 150 pages. Seven hundred copies were prepared for distribution to the many officers involved in the attack. The plan was issued on 5 November.

Meanwhile, on 5 October, about a hundred carrier pilots were called to a meeting on the *Akagi* in Shibushi Bay. Yamamoto described the plan to them, and told them that although Japan had never wanted to fight the United States, she was forced to because otherwise the country would be defeated if the United States continued its aid to China and maintained the oil embargo. Yamamoto told them that the U.S. fleet was Japan's strongest enemy; if they could strike it unexpectedly at Hawaii, by the time the fleet was ready to maneuver again Japan would have occupied Borneo, the Philippines, Singapore, Java and Sumatra.

The various ships first assembled in Kure and Yokosuka. The surface combatant ships left Kure, in several small groups, commencing on 10 November. The last group sailed on 18 November, and by 22 November they were all in Tankan Bay. Not until that time were the crews informed as to the purpose of the task force. The submarines sailed from Kure and Yokosuka between November 18 and 20. They refueled at Kwajalein in the Marshall Islands, and then headed for their assigned stations in Hawaiian waters.

In Tokyo on 21 November, Imperial General Headquarters issued Navy Order No. 5 which, in effect, told Admiral Yamamoto to direct his forces to proceed as planned. On 25 November Yamamoto, aboard the flagship *Nagato* in Hiroshima, ordered Admiral Nagumo, Commander Pearl Harbor Attack Force, to get his force underway on 26 November. The task force sailed at 6 a.m. the next morning, en route to a point about a thousand miles north of Hawaii, where the ships would refuel. The *Soryu* and *Hiryu,* in particular, had low fuel capacity; they both carried hundreds of drums of oil on deck, and their last fueling was by sailors forming bucket brigades to pour the stuff into fuel tanks.

The weather was bad, as the Japanese had expected, and this helped to hide the movements of such a large force from any chance ship. The ships sailed at 14 knots, to save fuel, with three submarines scouting 200 miles ahead in order to warn of any ships in the path.

The attack date was set for 8 December, Japanese time, which was 7 December, U.S. time. With careful observance of the letter of international law which holds that it is legal to declare war even though the declaration

As the Japanese carriers worked up to top speed, flight deck crews made final preparations to launch aircraft.

precedes actual hostilities by only a minute, Japan planned to have her diplomats in Washington deliver a declaration of war at exactly 1 p.m., Sunday. The time then in Hawaii would be 7:30 a.m., sufficient advance warning to nicely satisfy international law.

However, in the event negotiations in Washington went to Japan's satisfaction, the attack could still be called off. On 30 November, in Washington, Japan's negotiator's, Nomura and Kurusu, rejected the U.S. proposals for settling the crisis. The decision to go to war was made in Tokyo at an Imperial Conference on 1 December. The attack force, the next day, received a coded message: "Climb Mount Niitaka" which meant that the attack was still on and the time, 7 December in Hawaii, had been firmly settled.

A couple of days later, the tankers refueled the screening ships and then turned back toward Japan. The task force then increased speed to 24 knots. The day before the attack was due, the submarine *I-72* reported that the U.S. fleet was not in Lahaina Roads, the sheltered anchorage off Maui. This meant it was either in Pearl Harbor, and bottled up, or at sea where it might not be located. However, intelligence reports from Tokyo were able to give the attacking ships a fairly accurate and up-to-date plan of where the fleet really was, and the last one received indicated that at least 40 units of the fleet were in Pearl Harbor. The last night out, just to make certain that nothing had leaked and the Americans were not expecting them, Lieutenant Commander Kanjiro Ono, aboard the *Akagi,* fiddled with his radio all night, checking stations in Honolulu. KGMB kept right on playing Hawaiian music.

The next morning, 7 December, Hawaiian time, the cruisers *Tone* and *Chikuma* each catapulted a float plane, to go ahead and scout out the actual location of the U.S. fleet. The six carriers turned into the wind and began launching aircraft. "Hawaii Operation" was on.

First Enemy Contacts

(This section describes actions by the U.S. Navy on 7 December, and Navy time is used).

In the early morning hours of Sunday, 7 December 1941, four small minesweepers, *Condor, Crossbill, Cockatoo,* and *Reedbird* were making a routine sweep for magnetic mines off the Pearl Harbor channel entrance. The old destroyer *Ward* was also on patrol in the area. The only other naval vessels underway in the immediate area were the *Antares,* nearing Oahu with a 500-ton barge she had towed up from Palmyra, the *Keosanqua,* waiting outside the entrance to take over the barge, and the *Navajo,* about 12 miles outside the channel entrance and on her way in. The sequence of events for the remaining peaceful hours of that day were as follows:

0342 *Condor* bridge watch, consisting of Ensign R. C. McCloy, Quartermaster Second Class R. C. Uttrick, and Seaman First Class R. B. Chaves, spotted a submarine about 50 yards off the bow of the ship, headed for the entrance to Pearl Harbor. The *Condor* notified the *Ward* by yardarm blinker: SIGHTED SUBMARINE ON WESTERLY COURSE SPEED FIVE KNOTS.

Japanese fleet submarines launched their piggy-back two-man subs early on Sunday morning, then moved to take positions to intercept US ships leaving Pearl Harbor.

0458 Submarine net gate opened to allow *Condor* to enter channel.

0508 *Crossbill* entered channel. The gate remained open for *Antares.*

0600 *Enterprise,* still 200 miles west of Oahu, launched 18 aircraft which would scout ahead of her, then land on Ford Island.

0630 *Antares* approached net gate, and Seaman H. E. Raenbig, in the *Ward,* spotted something in water astern of the ship. At the same time PBY 14-P-1 piloted by Ensign William Tanner began circling the object. The *Ward*'s officer of the deck, Lieutenant (jg) Oscar Goepner, immediately called his skipper, Lieutenant William W. Outerbridge, to the bridge.

0640 *Ward* sounded general quarters.

0645 *Ward* opened fire on the suspicious object at a range of 100 yards. The first shot of the war was fired by number 1 gun, with Boatswain's Mate A. Art as gun captain. Number 1 gun missed on the first shot, but number 3 gun, with Russell Knapp as gun captain, hit the conning tower. On signal from the bridge, Chief Torpedoman W. C. Maskeawitcz dropped four depth charges. The PBY pilot, Ensign Tanner, also dropped depth charges.

0653 *Ward* sent radio message to Commandant, Fourteenth Naval District: WE HAVE ATTACKED FIRED UPON AND DROPPED DEPTH CHARGES UPON SUBMARINE OPERATING IN DEFENSIVE SEA AREA. The water there was 1,200 feet deep. The submarine did not come up.

0702 Army radar station at Opana, manned by Privates George E. Elliott and Joseph L. Lockard, picked up a "target," a large group of airplanes 132 miles distant, bearing 003 degrees, and closing at about 180 miles an hour.

Typical flight deck scene aboard a Japanese aircraft carrier, with plane handlers crouching under wings to keep clear of spinning props as engines warm up prior to take-off. **IJN Photo.**

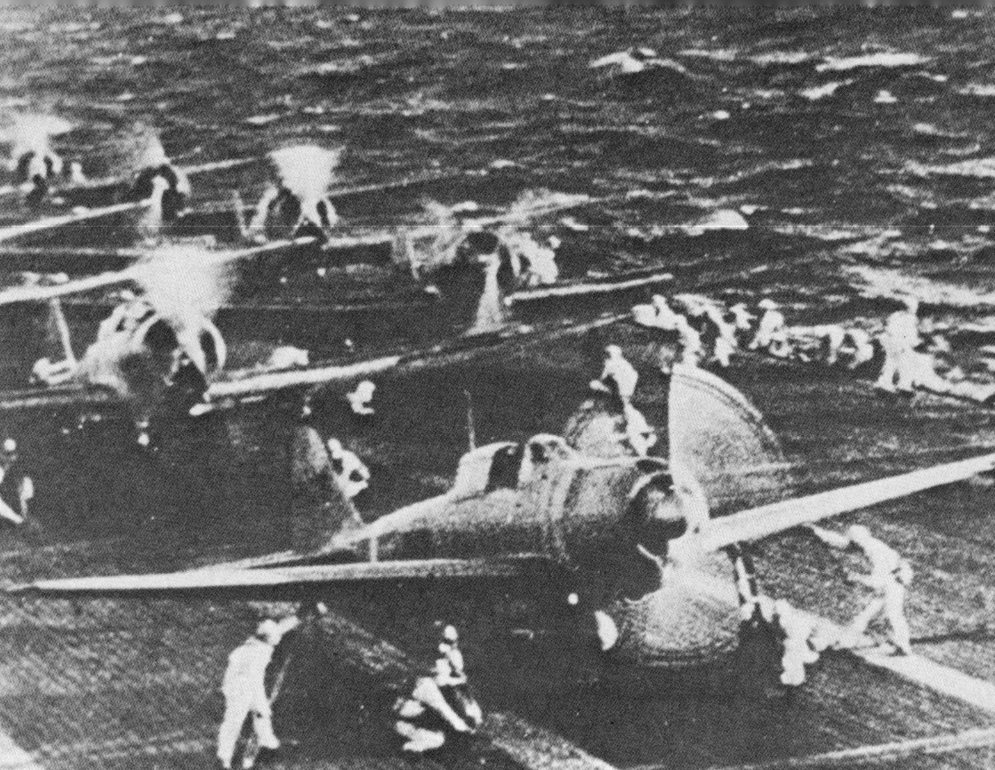

Actual view of Japanese planes just before take-off the morning of 7 December. Note early morning shadows. **IJN Photo.**

0715 The *Ward*'s attack message, transmitted at 0653, and delayed in decoding, was delivered to the Duty officer, Fourteenth Naval District.

0716 The same message was delivered to the Duty Officer, Commander-in-Chief, U.S. Fleet.

0720 Private Lockard informed the watch officer at Fort Shafter of his aircraft contact. No action was taken there, possibly because a large group of Army B-17's were expected in from California at about that time. (*Note:* there was no radar watch maintained in Pearl Harbor. Many ships, including battleships and destroyers, had radar installed by late 1941, but the sets could not be used because the high mountains around the harbor blocked their transmissions.)

0725 Commander Fourteenth Naval District ordered ready duty destroyer *Monaghan* to get underway, investigate submarine contact reported by *Ward.*

0741 Headquarters office of Commander in Chief Pacific Fleet at Submarine Base received PBY report on bombing submarine. Message had been logged in at 0700 but delayed in decoding.

0751 *Monaghan* received message released by Commander Fourteenth Naval District at 0725.

First attacking torpedo planes came in low over Merry Point, past the end of 1010 dock, headed for battleship row.

0755 Signal tower at Navy Yard hoisted PREP, signal to all ships in harbor to "make colors" at 0800. The only ship not at anchor, the destroyer *Helm,* was turning up the channel to West Loch when some planes flew past, very low. A pilot waved at the ship, and Quartermaster Frank Handler waved back. Seconds later a bomb hit in the Patrol Squadron 22 parking area on Ford Island and fire and smoke went up. The Navy Yard signal tower put out the first word: ENEMY AIR RAID NOT DRILL.

0758 Commander Patrol Wing Two broadcast a radio message: AIR RAID PEARL HARBOR THIS IS NO DRILL.

On some ships, as men saw the smoke from burning planes on Ford Island, and heard the general alarms sound, they assumed they were being called away for a "fire and rescue party." Not until they heard machine gun bullets whining around them, or actually saw bombs and torpedoes dropping, did they realize they were at war. One man who did not realize this until too late was Ensign Manual Gonzales, an *Enterprise* pilot on his way in to Ford Island. At 0800 other *Enterprise* pilots heard him exclaim "Don't shoot; I'm a friendly plane." His voice was never heard again, and his plane was never found.

A few savvy sailors, and particularly some who had seen the Japanese at war in China, recognized the red "meat balls" on the planes as Japanese insignia and didn't wait for orders. They had their machine guns loaded and firing even

as other men on the ships "made colors" in the customary manner at eight o'clock. On the *Nevada,* the band played the "Star Spangled Banner," like always, all the way through, before they broke and ran.

By that time, the war was on, all around Pearl Harbor. Several thousand miles away in Washington, D.C., the time was 1:30 p.m. Japanese diplomats Kichisaburo Nomura and Saburo Kurusu were to have met with Secretary of State Cordell Hull at 1 p.m. and deliver the message which would inform the United States that Japan was at war, but the Japanese had had difficulty decoding their own message, and asked a delay until 1:45 p.m. When they finally arrived at 2:05 p.m., Hull had already read the message, decoded earlier by U.S. experts. Instead of giving the U.S. the 30 minutes advance warning they had planned, the Japanese came to announce a war which had already been going on for 35 minutes.

Chronology of the Japanese Attack on Hawaii

(Based on an account by CDR. Mitsuo Fuchida, Imperial Japanese Navy)

0530 *Tone* and *Chikuma,* heavy cruisers, each catapulted one Zero float plane for reconnaissance flights—the *Chikuma* plane to fly over Pearl Harbor, the *Tone* plane to fly over Lahaina Roads, where the fleet sometimes anchored. At that time the task force was 230 miles due north of Oahu.

0600 Carriers began launching first attack wave, of 183 fighters, bombers, and torpedo planes. In fifteen minutes all planes were aloft.

***The opening moment of the attack, as an explosion lifts a tower of water several hundred feet above the* Maryland *and* Oklahoma. IJN Photo.**

0615 Attack wave headed south for Oahu.

0700 Commander Fuchida estimated flight would arrive over Oahu a bit sooner than planned due to a tail wind. He tuned in a Honolulu radio station and got a radio bearing, and at the time a weather report: "Averaging partly cloudy, with clouds mostly over the mountains. Cloud base at 3500 feet. Visibility good. Wind north, 10 knots."

0740 Fuchida fired his signal pistol once; "one black dragon" meant the force would make a surprise attack. By that time, the *Chikuma* reconnaissance plane reported ten battleships, one heavy cruiser, and ten light cruisers in Pearl Harbor. The *Tone* plane reported no ships at Lahaina.

0749 Fuchida ordered his radioman to send the signal for all planes to launch attacks: "To, to, to, to . . ." The dive-bombers, led by Commander Takahashi, headed for Ford Island and Hickam Field; the second group of dive bombers led by Lieutenant Sakamoto headed for Wheeler Field. The torpedo bombers, led by Commander Murata, took a short cut to avoid smoke from fires at Hickam and hit battleship row five minutes earlier than originally scheduled.

0755 Dive bombers hit Hickam and Wheeler.

0757 Torpedo planes hit battleship row.

0800 Fighters began strafing various air bases.

0805 High-level horizontal bombers hit battleship row.

***Looking directly down on battleship row, as oil spreads over the water. At upper right,* Oklahoma *is rolling over alongside* Maryland. West Virginia *is on fire outboard of* Tennessee. *Next left is* Vestal *with* Arizona *inboard;* Nevada *at far left is barely visible.* IJN Photo.**

***Two torpedo tracks can be seen in center of picture, and* West Virginia *is listing to port. Smoke in distance is from burning planes at Hickam Field.* IJN Photo.**

The only aircraft in the air were Japanese, the ships in the harbor had not opened fire, and the Honolulu radio stations were still on the air. Fuchida then had his radioman transmit the code signal for a successful surprise attack: "TORA, TORA, TORA . . ."

By the time Fuchida had signalled his level bombers into a column formation for their attack, antiaircraft fire spotted the sky. Shipboard guns were firing less than five minutes after the first bomb drop, a fact which surprised the Japanese. On the bombing run, Fuchida's plane was hit, but only slightly damaged. Some planes had to make three attempts on a bombing run before they got past the AA barrage and could drop their bombs. As he circled, Fuchida saw the *Arizona* explode in a thousand-foot high column of dark red smoke; the shock wave of the explosion shook his plane.

The smoke from the *Arizona* hid the *Nevada,* so Fuchida looked for another target. The *Tennessee* was on fire, so he headed for the *Maryland,* dropped four bombs, and saw two big rings in the water alongside the ship, meaning two misses, but the other two were hits.

With the bombing run completed, Fuchida ordered his planes to strafe air bases, while he circled Pearl Harbor to check damage. The *Utah* capsized, *Maryland* and *Tennessee* were burning, and only the *Pennsylvania,* in dry dock, seemed undamaged. At 1010 Dock, the *Helena* and *Oglala* were damaged.

The aircraft in the first attack wave were over the harbor for about an hour. Before they left, a few American aircraft came up to engage them* and the Japanese admired their courage in attacking although greatly outnumbered.

0840 The second Japanese attack wave of 171 aircraft led by Lieutenant Commander Shimazaki arrived over Kahuku Point.

0854 Attack run began, with thirty-six fighters remaining over Pearl Harbor to maintain air control, fifty-four high-level bombers attacking NAS Kaneohe and Hickam Field under the leadership of Shimazaki, and eighty-one dive bombers under Lieutenant Commander Egusa returning to hit ships in Pearl Harbor.

That attack also lasted about an hour, but targets were obscured by smoke, and the antiaircraft fire was so intense by that time that the Japanese casualties were much heavier—twenty planes shot down as compared to the loss of only nine during the first attack.

1100 Fuchida left the Pearl Harbor area to return to his carrier. During the attack the carriers had moved in to a point only 190 miles from Oahu, to help those planes which were short on fuel.

1300 Fuchida landed aboard *Akagi.* He was the last pilot to return from the Pearl Harbor attack. Aircraft were already spotted for take-off on a second strike. Fuchida urged Admiral Nagumo to launch another attack, but he declined. Probably his prime reason for this was that the raid had proved there were no aircraft carriers in Pearl Harbor, although the Japanese well knew a couple of carriers were operating out of Hawaii, and without knowing exactly where they were, Nagumo did not choose to find himself on the receiving end of a surprise attack such as he had just successfully completed. The matter was settled by Admiral Kusaka, the Chief of Staff, who said "The attack is terminated. We are withdrawing."

1330 The Japanese attack force changed course and began its return to Japan.

Target A

The two-man, midget submarines used in the attack were designated by the Japanese as Target A. Twenty of them had been built, and five were transported to the Hawaiian area by large ocean-going I-class submarines. The plan laid down in "Hawaii Operation" called for them to wait outside the harbor until the air attack commenced, then if possible to move inside and launch torpedoes. The Japanese had been developing the little craft ever since the idea was first suggested in 1933. Not all senior naval officers favored the plan; in operation, it was a complete failure.

The mother subs—I-16, I-18, I-20, I-22 and I-24—each carrying a midget—16-A, 18-A, 20-A, 22-A and 24-A—clamped to their topside, piggyback fashion, left Kure on 18 November. The midget submarines were to be launched very early on the morning of 7 December, off the Pearl Harbor entrance; I-24 had to delay launching her midget for about two hours because it had compass trouble. By the time 24-A was on its way, the first midget had already been sunk by the

* These were from the aircraft carrier *Enterprise.*

Ward, off the channel entrance. With a faulty compass, 24-A got lost; the first thing Ensign Kazuo Sakamaki knew, he was aground on a reef where the destroyer *Helm* saw the sub as she came charging out of the harbor about 0830 that morning. Then he got off, and wandered around for hours until he finally went aground again. That time he and his assistant abandoned the sub to swim ashore. The other man drowned, but Sakamaki made it to a beach near Bellows Field. There he was captured by Sergeant David Akui, which gave him the dubious honor of becoming Japanese prisoner of war number 1.

At least one of the midgets made it into Pearl Harbor, and cruised nearly all the way around Ford Island until it was spotted, about 0830, by the *Breese* and *Curtiss.* Several ships began firing at it. The *Curtiss* put a shot through the conning tower. The *Monaghan,* heading out the channel, fired on the sub, tried to ram it, and dropped depth charges to sink it.

After the war, the wreckage of the submarine was raised. The bodies of two crewmen were still trapped in it, so that section of the craft was cut out, and they were given a ceremonial burial. The Submarine Base, at that time, was building a new dock and needed fill material—the hull of the submarine was hauled there and covered with concrete.

Another midget submarine evidently lurked around outside until mid-morning, then fired two torpedoes at the *St. Louis* as she came out. That was a mistake—the torpedoes missed but the *St. Louis* gunners didn't.

One of the midgets was still on the prowl late Sunday night. A last radio message from it was received by a mother ship about 10:30 p.m. What happened to it after that is not known.

Several midget submarines have been preserved and are on display. One raised outside the Pearl Harbor channel in 1968, is at the Japanese Naval Academy at Eta Jima.

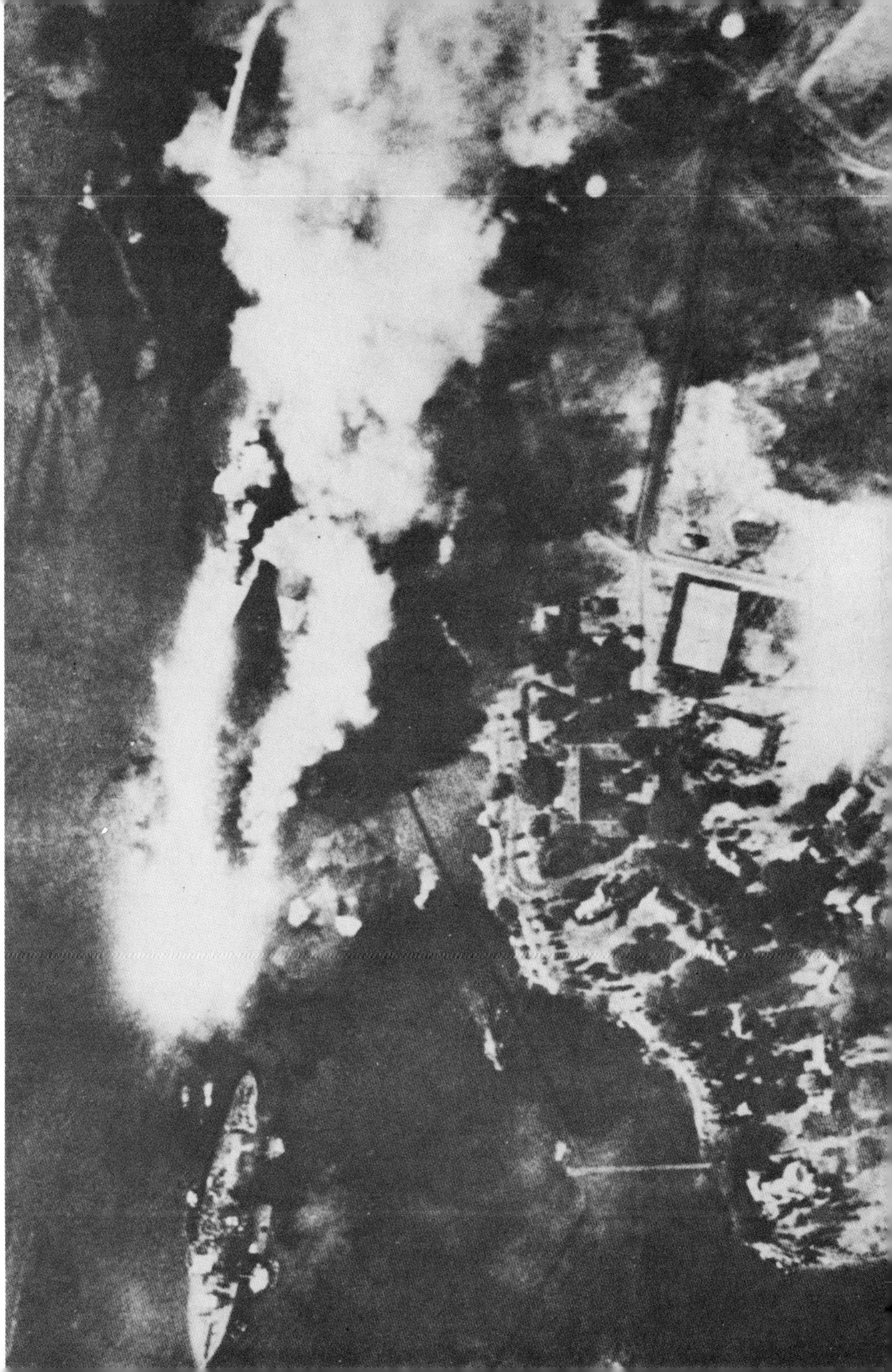

***As the* Arizona *blew up, smoke towered a thousand feet into the air and blotted out Ford Island. Motor launches can be seen circling about near the* Oklahoma. IJN Photo.**

On the first Anniversary of the attack on Pearl Harbor, Japan issued a stamp bearing a photo of the attack, made at almost the same instant as the photo on page 11.

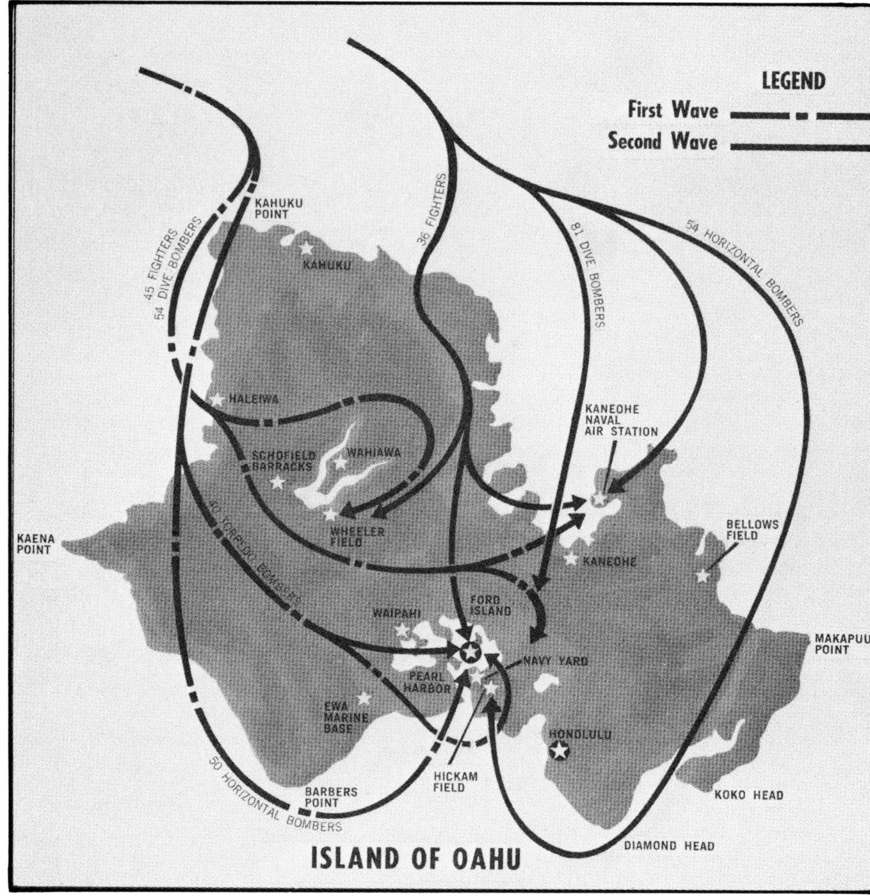

The island of Oahu, showing routes taken by the attacking Japanese aircraft.

ATTACK — U.S. ACCOUNT

The first warning any American had of the disaster about to strike Pearl Harbor was the sudden appearance of Japanese aircraft, flying low and fast over Merry Point and toward Ford Island. Because men were on deck on every ship in the harbor, the planes were seen almost simultaneously by literally hundreds of people, and because the planes had pre-selected targets which they hit at almost the same time, the war actually started all over the place, all at once. It is impossible for any one account of the action to cover what happened in Pearl Harbor in the next couple of hours. What follows here is a very brief description of the overall attack, with accounts of individual actions by those ships which were sunk or badly damaged.

The entire action lasted about an hour and fifty minutes, during which there were three concentrated attacks; it is officially described as consisting of these five phases:

I Concentrated attack by perhaps sixty-six torpedo bombers, dive-bombers and horizontal bombers, lasting from 0755 to 0825.

II Sporadic attacks by about fifteen dive-bombers, from 0825 to 0840.

III Heavy attack by an estimated forty-eight horizontal bombers, lasting from 0840 to 0915.

IV Dive-bombers, estimated at about twenty-seven, engaged in strafing from 0915 to 0945.

V All planes withdrew from attack, returned to carriers.

In the first phase, about nine dive bombers hit the Naval Air Station on Ford Island; they concentrated on planes parked near hangar no. 6, and practically wiped out the entire strength of Patrol Squadron 22 in the first minute. There was no further attack on Ford Island during the day. Except for a direct hit on the hangar by a bomb which had been aimed at the *California* and fell short. Damage to the station was light, but thirty-three out of seventy Navy planes of all types there were destroyed or damaged.

Admiral Husband E. Kimmel, the Commander in Chief, U.S. Pacific Fleet, in conference with Captain W. S. Delaney, Operations Officer, and Captain William W. Smith, Chief of Staff, late in 1941.

Battleship row on Saturday forenoon, 6 December.

At approximately the same time the planes hit Ford Island, other planes attacked the Kaneohe Naval Air Station, where they destroyed seaplanes moored in the bay. The first attack there lasted about ten to fifteen minutes. About half an hour later more planes hit Kaneohe in a bombing and strafing attack. A direct hit destroyed no. 3 hangar and four planes inside. Only nine out of thirty-six planes at Kaneohe escaped destruction; six of them were damaged and the others were on patrol south of Oahu.

The Marine Base at Ewa was hit in an attack commencing about two minutes before the planes hit Pearl Harbor. Two squadrons of single-seater fighters strafed, flying across the field at twenty to twenty-five feet, then pulling up to reverse direction and come back again. Inside of fifteen minutes, every Marine tactical aircraft had been shot up or set on fire. Then the fighters strafed Navy utility aircraft, disassembled planes, and men trying to set up machine guns. In only a few minutes, thirty-three of Ewa's forty-nine planes had gone up in smoke. The remaining planes were too shot-up to fly, so Marines fired at the attacking planes with pistols.

Although Pearl Harbor was hit first by dive bombers, it was the torpedo planes which did the most damage. They made four distinct attacks, generally coming in over Merry Point and the tank farm, and coming down practically "on the deck" to launch torpedoes. The outboard battleships—those in battleship row nearest the channel side—were hit first; these were the *Arizona, California, Oklahoma, Nevada* and *West Virginia.* All were damaged or sunk.

The *Arizona* was out of the fight almost before it started. She took several torpedoes and at least a couple of bombs before a high level bomber put one into her near the number 2 turret which blew up the forward magazines. The ship went down so fast she did not have time to roll over. Over a thousand men died in the minute that the ship blew up; a few hundred others had the sort of luck that comes only once in a lifetime.

In the second torpedo plane attack, three torpedoes hit the *Oklahoma* and she went over about 25 to 35 degrees. Men abandoned ship, scrambling over her starboard side as she rolled. Then two more torpedoes hit the ship and within twenty minutes from the time the attack opened, she had rolled over about 150 degrees, until her masts hit the bottom and stopped the roll. Men who could manage it climbed aboard the *Maryland,* alongside, to work on her antiaircraft guns. The *Oklahoma* lost about 315 officers and men.

The *Maryland,* moored inboard where torpedoes couldn't reach her, was lucky; the Japanese very nearly missed her. She took one small bomb on the forecastle which did little damage, and another armor-piercing type which exploded in a hold. A seaman machine gunner on the ship knocked down one torpedo plane even before it dropped its torpedo. The *Maryland* had only four officers and men killed or missing.

KEY

① Condor
Crossbill
Ash
PY109

② Vireo
Turkey
Bobolink
Rail

③ Shaw
Sotoyomo

④ Drydock No. 2

⑤ Drydock No. 1 Downes
Cassin
Pennsylvania

⑥ YR22
Cachalot

⑦ Oglala
Helena

⑧ Dredge Turbine

⑨ Avocet

⑩ Gasoline Wharf

⑪ Tern
YO30

⑫ Argonne
Jarvis
Mugford
Sacramento

⑬ Marine Railway SWAN (on Ry.)

⑭ Yard Craft Area:
YTT3
YT129
YT142
YT146
YT119
YT130
YT152
YG15
Sunnadin

⑮ YG21

⑯ Ramapo

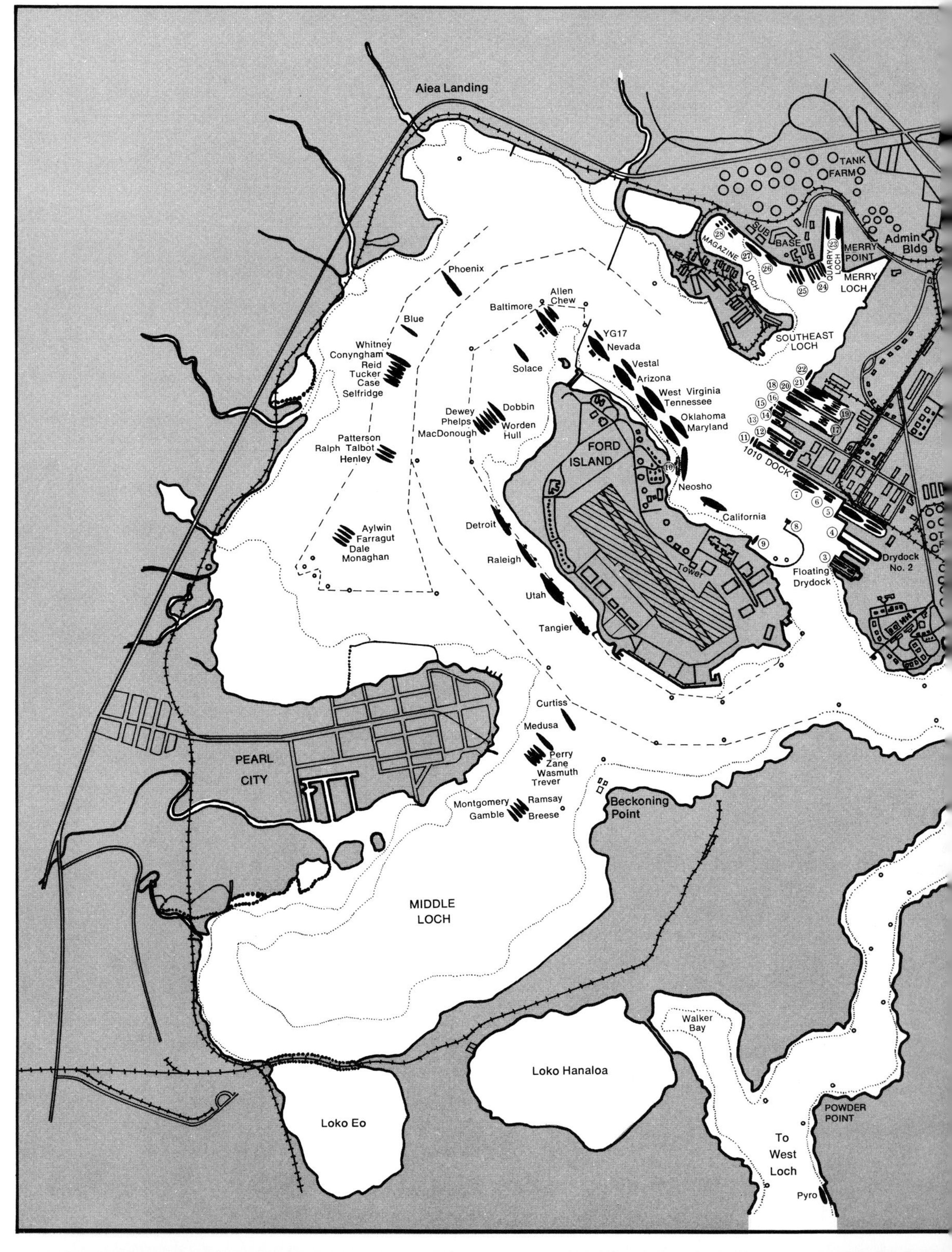

in preparation of this chart provided by the PEARL
SURVIVORS ASSOCIATION through Historian Robert A.

PEARL HARBOR
7 December 1941

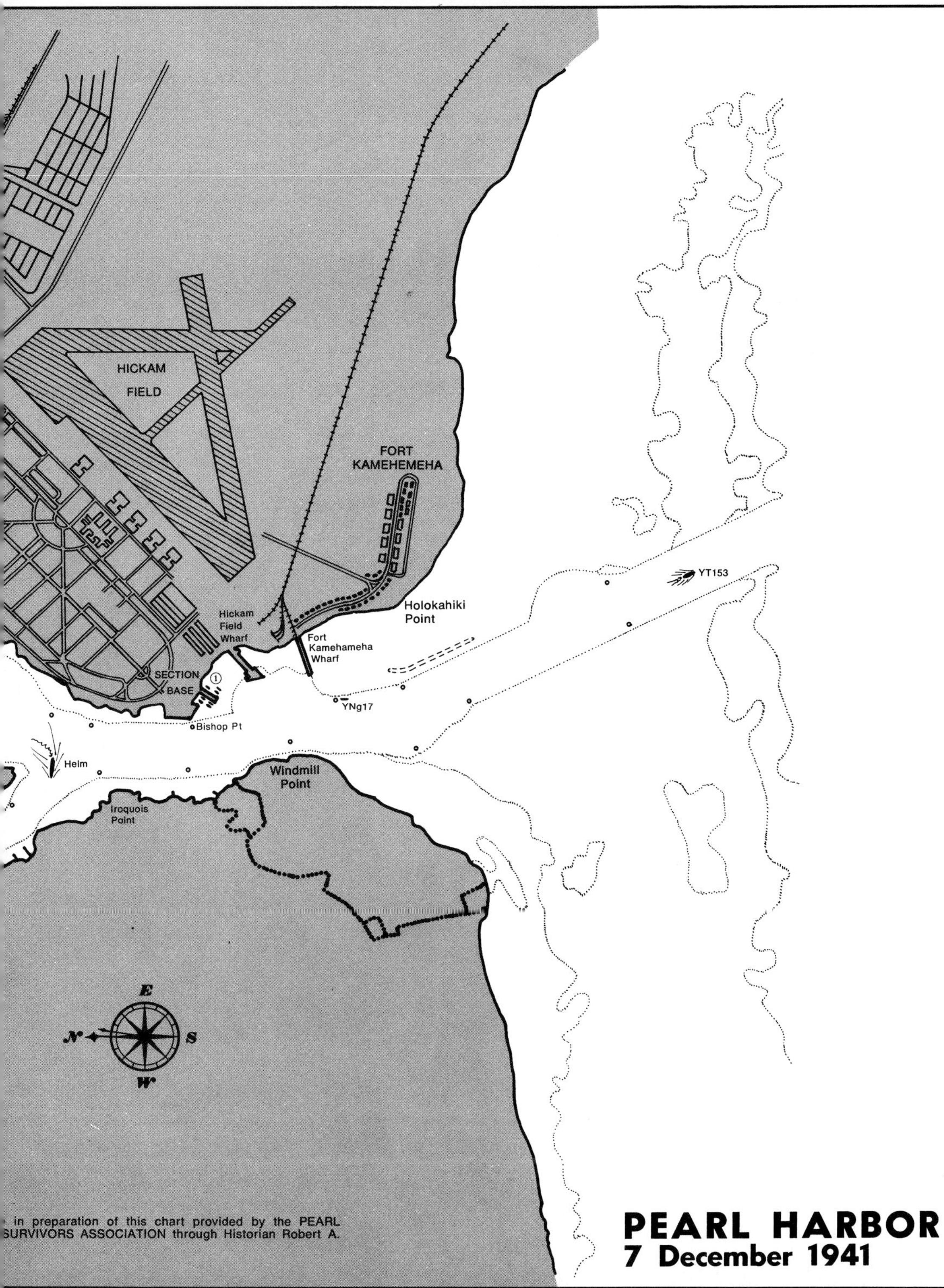

KEY

⑰ Rigel
Cummings
Preble
Tracy

⑱ New Orleans

⑲ Pruitt
Sicard
Ontario
Grebe
Schley

⑳ San Francisco

㉑ St. Louis
Honolulu

㉒ Bagley

㉓ Castor
Sumner

㉔ Tautog
Hulbert
Thornton

㉕ YO
Narwhal
Dolphin

㉖ Widgeon

㉗ Pelios

㉘ PT25
YR20

PT23
PT21

PT24
PT20
PT22

Note: PT26 and 28 on dock under crane.
PT27, 29, 30 and 42 on Ramapo.

NOTES:

1. USS Ward DD139 steaming on Channel Entrance Patrol off Pearl Harbor.
2. USS Antares AKS3 steaming single en route Palmyra Island to Pearl Harbor with HDS2 Lighter in tow. Advised Ward of suspicious object.
3. USS Keosanqua AT38 underway at 0610 from Berth B-9 to receive Antares tow.
4. USS Vega AK17 moored starboard side to Pier 31A Honolulu Harbor.
5. USCG R. B. Taney moored at Pier 6 Honolulu Harbor.
6. USCG Reliance moored at Pier 4 Honolulu Harbor.
7. USCG Tiger PC152 patrolling off Barbers Point.
8. USS Cockenoe YN47 Honolulu Harbor Net Tender.
9. At Section Base: USS Marin Yn53, Wapello, YMT5, Chenango, YN47. (Exact locations not known.)

Fierce antiaircraft fire met the later high-level bomber attacks. This photo, made about 0845, shows smoke from fires at the Navy Yard, left, and from burning battleships, right. The* Neosho *is underway, lower left.

In the third attack, one lone torpedo plane aimed at the cruiser *Helena,* moored at 1010 dock. The mine layer *Oglala* was moored outboard of the *Helena,* but the torpedo ran underneath her and hit the *Helena* in her engine room. Although the torpedo missed and hit the *Helena, Oglala* got the worst of it; the force of the explosion against the *Helena* ruptured her old sides—she had been built in 1906—and then a bomb dropped between the two ships and she lost all power. With the aid of a couple of passing tugs, her crew moved the ship to the dock astern of the *Helena,* where she continued to flood, and about two hours after the attack began she rolled over.

The fourth attack wave came in over Pearl City and Middle Loch, and hit the ships moored on the opposite side of Ford Island from battleship row. When carriers were in port, they secured there, and the old *Utah,* converted to an aerial target ship, looked enough like an aircraft carrier to get special attention. Two torpedoes into her started her over, and she capsized at 0813. The cruiser *Raleigh,* in another berth, also took a torpedo and started to roll over; her crew put out extra lines to the quays and literally held her upright until the battle was over; they threw overboard aircraft, lockers, and everything they could pry loose to make her lighter—but kept notes on where the stuff dropped so they could get it again later.

The *Detroit* and *Tangier* had ringside seats at the biggest fight they had ever seen, and didn't get touched. The *Detroit* got underway later and was outside the harbor by mid-day, to meet the *Enterprise.*

Other planes in the third attack wave hit the battleship *West Virginia*—she took two bombs, which were duds, and so many torpedoes that at least a couple of them came in through holes made by others which hit first. One knocked her rudder off; it was picked up off the bottom later. The crew fought fires for thirty hours; as soon as they got one out more burning oil from the wreck of the *Arizona* would come in through torpedo holes and start another.

Most of the torpedo damage to the fleet had occurred by 0825. The *California, Oklahoma, West Virginia* and *Nevada* had been hit, the *Arizona* was a raging fire, the *California* was sinking, and the *Oklahoma* was upside down. The *Nevada* had been torpedoed once, but was still afloat and making preparations for that classic naval maneuver known as "getting the hell out of here."

While the Japanese had had a busy half hour, the U.S. Navy had also been busy. Machine guns on many ships had started firing as soon as the first bombs dropped, and within five minutes after the attack began, practically every antiaircraft gun in the harbor was firing. The *Nevada* got at least two planes in the opening minutes of the battle, and the *Tangier* got another. The old seaplane tender *Avocet* got one of the planes that torpedoed the *California.* Gun crews on the destroyers, which were not quite so busy dodging torpedoes and bombs as they were on the larger ships, shot at everything which came their way, and splashed a few planes.

During phase 2, which was termed a lull in the action, there were only scattered attacks by about fifteen dive-bombers and horizontal bombers. During that period, there was a minor one-sided action in the channel between Ford

The* Nevada, *aground off Waipio Point. A yard tug off the port bow is fighting fire. Irregular paint along the starboard side is a bow wave painted as a form of camouflage.

Island and Pearl City when a midget submarine was sunk. (*See section titled* Weapon A. *A photograph of that submarine, when raised, appears on page 27.*)

In the third phase of the attack, about thirty high-level bombers crossed and recrossed the harbor at 10,000 feet, high enough so the AA guns had little success in reaching them, and dropped bombs along battleship row and in the Navy Yard. Some eighteen dive-bombers also took part in that attack. The *California* was hit by a bomb which exploded on the second deck and started a fire. She had been preparing for a material inspection, and many watertight manhole covers had been removed, so water and in some cases oil gradually found its way into parts of the ship which were ordinarily sealed tight. The ship sank, very slowly; after three days she was on the bottom, with water over the port side forward and over the after turret. She was refloated in March, 1942.

The *Curtiss,* which had helped sink a submarine earlier, had a bomb hit on her main deck which killed twenty men and wounded fifty-eight others. She then fired on another bomber pulling out of a dive over the Naval Air Station and set it on fire; the plane in turn hit the *Curtiss* and started several gasoline fires.

As bombers in the third attack generally concentrated on the battleships and the Navy Yard, other ships began hauling clear of the area. The *Neosho,* caught between the *California* on one side and the *Maryland* and *Oklahoma* on the other, and loaded with oil, pulled out at 0842 and headed toward Merry Point, to clear the way in case the *Maryland* could get out. The *Vestal,* bombed by the Japanese and on fire from the *Arizona*'s burning oil, got underway at almost the same instant. She was down by the stern and in danger of sinking, so her captain beached her over near Aiea. By that time a few destroyers were getting underway—the *Blue, Dale, Aylwin, Henley,* and *Phelps*—and as the third attack phase ended, the cruiser *St. Louis* backed clear of her Navy Yard berth and started out. Just outside the channel entrance, two torpedoes were fired at her by one of the midget submarines. *St. Louis* fired on it and probably accounted for the fourth one of the five lost by the Japanese that morning.

West Virginia *sitting on the bottom, with* Tennessee *inboard. Mine-sweeper* Tern *is fighting fire. Note mine-sweeping paravanes stowed on number 2 turret, and SK radar antenna on foremast.*

Against a background of smoke from the* Arizona, *the* Neosho *backs clear of her berth, past* Maryland *and* Tennessee. *Hull of the capsized* Oklahoma *just aft of* Neosho. California *at left.

During the third phase of the attack, the *Nevada* got underway and was heading seaward, past 1010 dock. Dive bombers made a determined effort to stop her—a ship sunk in the channel would bottle up the entire harbor. With her bridge and superstructure in flames from several bomb hits, she moved down the channel, an inspiring sight to men whose ships were out of the fight and could do nothing about the Japanese except swear at them. Finally, in fear that the Japanese still might sink the ship, she was deliberately put aground at Waipio Point.

On the Navy Yard side of the channel, the destroyer *Shaw* was in Floating Dry Dock No. 2, along with the little tug, *Sotoyomo.* The *Shaw* was in a precarious situation—high and dry, with her ammunition still on board. A bomb, possibly intended for the *Nevada,* hit the *Shaw* and started a fire. Sailors fought it as long as they could, until the heat set her forward magazines off in an explosion that wrecked the ship, sank the dock, and threw a five-inch shell clear across the channel to Ford Island.

In the big Dry Dock No. 1 at the Navy Yard, the Pacific fleet flagship, *Pennsylvania,* was also high and dry on the keel blocks, along with destroyers *Cassin* and *Downes.* The three ships were in a handy spot for dive bombers and fighters finishing a pass at Hickam Field—they could take a shot at the drydocked ships without turning around. The *Pennsylvania* began firing almost at once; the destroyers had to wait until sailors could scurry to a shop in the yard for missing gun parts, but they were firing before the first attack phase ended.

The same planes that tried to stop the *Nevada* in her seaward dash also worked over ships in the Navy Yard. Soon after the *Shaw* blew up, a bomb hit between *Cassin* and *Downes.* With the ships out of the water, their oil tanks were ruptured and a raging oil fire soon forced the crews to abandon ship. About that time the *Pennsylvania* was hit, and her captain ordered the dry dock flooded to put out the fires around *Cassin* and *Downes.* The burning oil merely floated on top of the water and came up with it. Finally the heat set off the magazines in the two destroyers, and the explosion in the *Cassin* tumbled her over onto the *Downes.*

Simultaneously with the attack on Pearl Harbor, at least a hundred other planes hit Army air fields at Hickam, Wheeler and Bellows Field. As usual, aircraft had been parked wing tip to wing tip, in parallel rows, as a means of preventing sabotage, and this made it a simple matter to strafe and bomb several on a single firing run. Hickam underwent three attacks, in which at least eighteen out of fifty-six bombers were destroyed. The Japanese also bombed a baseball diamond, possibly mistaking it for an underground fuel tank.

Wheeler Field, which handled mostly fighters, lost forty out of the hundred on the field. Bellows Field, with only twenty aircraft on hand, was hit lightly in strafing attacks, and lost two fighters and an observation plane.

Wreck of the Cassin *and* Downes *in Dry Dock No. 1. Superstructure of* Pennsylvania *visible at upper right, with antenna of SK radar atop foremast.*

View from the Submarine Base. Narwhal *at left, smoke from burning* Cassin *and* Downes *over her conning tower. Destroyer* Bagley *just behind the flag staff. Cruisers* Honolulu, St. Louis *and* San Francisco *in distance.*

Wreckage on Ford Island: Seagulls at left, a Kingfisher in center, wings and motor mounts of a Catalina visible over the Kingfisher.

Because some Japanese aircraft attacked at more than one point, and some appeared over Pearl Harbor several times, estimates of the numbers of planes making the attacks varied widely. The most accurate figure is that furnished by the Japanese after the war; they said that 183 planes were launched for the first wave and 171 were launched for the second wave, for a total of 354. The American estimates of the numbers of enemy aircraft shot down also varied widely. Again, the Japanese were in the best position to know; they counted the aircraft that returned from the raid. Twenty-nine of them never came back.

The Japanese succeeded, beyond their wildest dreams, in achieving complete surprise in their attack. The appearance of enemy aircraft over Pearl Harbor and the various air fields was so sudden and the bombs, fires, and explosions were so unexpected, that even as men watched they couldn't believe their eyes. Some thought the Japanese planes were merely U.S. planes disguised for a practice air raid. The first few bombs were also thought to be practice drops—and when a few planes on the ground blew up, someone decided that some U.S. pilot would catch hell for his mistake.

In the confusion of fire, explosions, and frantic efforts to put up antiaircraft barrages, rescue burned and drowning men, and fight fire and flood in bombed ships, improbable conjecture and impossible rumors were accepted as fact. Even before the first Japanese aircraft had left Pearl Harbor the word spread that they were already coming back . . . dozens of transports were unloading at Barbers Point . . . paratroopers were coming down all over the place . . . a bunch of Japanese battleships were nearing the island . . . saboteurs were busy wrecking planes, putting down signals in the cane fields, and dumping poison in the water supply.

People who hadn't yet seen a Japanese pilot heard that they had been shot down, wearing high school sweaters and college class rings from well known Hawaiian and stateside schools; others had heard that the *Pennsylvania* had captured and was towing in a couple of Japanese battleships—this despite the fact that the "Pennsy" was still in the Navy Yard drydock.

As the first terse radio announcements of the attack flashed across the mainland United States, they were received with disbelief, shock, and amazement. Only later did people begin to feel outrage, turn fighting mad, and go off to recruiting stations to sign up for the duration. The news from Hawaii was sketchy at best; immediately a tight censorship lid clamped down on almost everything issuing from Honolulu and Washington, but it in no way stopped speculation about what had happened. Obviously, officials didn't want to broadcast to the world the exact details on how much damage had been done to the fleet in Pearl Harbor. There was little chance that the Japanese might come back for another try, and no one knew this better than the Japanese who were hurrying home to the Empire—they had achieved their purpose. But just in case . . . there was no use letting them know there wasn't one battleship in Pearl Harbor ready to fight, there or anywhere else.

But in Hawaii, and elsewhere, in the eyes of timid, worried, and suddenly suspicious people, anything afloat in the Pacific, or in the air over the Pacific, looked like a Japanese ship or aircraft, and imaginations began working overtime. Somehow or other, the entire state of California was spooked on Monday night, and *Time* magazine reported as cold fact in its December 15 issue that

". . . right after sunset Monday the incredible happened again. San Francisco had a blackout and the Army announced that two squadrons of 15 enemy planes each from a carrier off the coast had flown over California soil near San Jose. One squadron flew south and vanished. The second flew northward past San Francisco and Mare Island.

They both made TIME. *Kimmel, 15 December and Yamamoto, 22 December.*

Covers reprinted by special permission of TIME, The Weekly Newsmagazine; © Time Inc., 1941.

Just after midnight the planes came back again, and before dawn there was a third alarm. Each time they flew high. They did not drop any bombs. . . ."

The reason being, there were no Japanese aircraft carriers anywhere within thousands of miles of the United States, and without carriers, there could be no aircraft to "not" drop bombs.

A week later *Time* printed another account of the Pearl Harbor attack, updated, as it were, to include the latest returns: "In all these were six separate attacks, the others coming in at 11:29, 11:59, 12:22 p.m., 7:15 and 9:10." No one in the United States Navy saw or heard the last five attacks, no one in the Japanese Navy ever admitted making them, and *Time* magazine never explained where all those imaginary aircraft over California and Hawaii came from.

The U.S. Declaration of War

Shortly before noon on 8 December, President Roosevelt addressed a joint session of Congress, as follows:

Yesterday, December 7, 1941—a date which will live in infamy—the United States of America was suddenly and deliberately attacked by naval and air forces of the Empire of Japan.

The United States was at peace with that Nation and, at the solicitation of Japan, was still in conversation with its Government and its Emperor looking toward the maintenance of peace in the Pacific. Indeed, one hour after Japanese air squadrons had commenced bombing in Oahu, the Japanese Ambassador to the United States and his colleague delivered to the Secretary of State a formal reply to a recent American message. While this reply stated that it seemed useless to continue the existing diplomatic negotiations, it contained no threat or hint of war or armed attack.

It will be recorded that the distance of Hawaii from Japan makes it obvious that the attack was deliberately planned many days or even weeks ago. During the intervening time the Japanese Government has deliberately sought to deceive the United States by false statements and expressions of hope for continued peace.

The attack yesterday on the Hawaiian Islands has caused severe damage to American naval and military forces. Very many American lives have been lost. In addition, American ships have been reported torpedoed on the high seas between San Francisco and Honolulu.

Yesterday the Japanese Government also launched an attack against Malaya.

Last night Japanese forces attacked Hong Kong.
Last night Japanese forces attacked Guam.
Last night Japanese forces attacked the Philippine Islands.
Last night the Japanese attacked Wake Island.
This morning the Japanese attacked Midway Island.

Japan has, therefore, undertaken a surprise offensive extending throughout the Pacific area. The facts of yesterday speak for themselves. The people

In the White House on 8 December 1941, President Franklin D. Roosevelt signed the U.S. declaration of war against Japan. Roosevelt did not live to see the war end; he died on 13 April 1945. **U.S. Army photo.**

of the United States have already formed their opinions and well understand the implications to the very life and safety of our Nation.

As Commander-in-Chief of the Army and Navy I have directed that all measures be taken for our defense.

Always will we remember the character of the onslaught against us.

No matter how long it may take us to overcome this premeditated invasion, the American people in their righteous might will win through to absolute victory.

I believe I interpret the will of the Congress and of the people when I assert that we will not only defend ourselves to the uttermost but will make very certain that this form of treachery shall never endanger us again.

Hostilities exist. There is no blinking at the fact that our people, our territory, and our interests are in grave danger.

With confidence in our armed forces—with the unbounded determination of our people—we will gain the inevitable triumph—so help us God.

I ask that the Congress declare that since the unprovoked and dastardly attack by Japan on Sunday, December seventh, a state of war has existed between the United States and the Japanese Empire.

Within an hour after the President finished his address, the Senate voted 82 to 0 and the House voted 388 to 1 to declare war on Japan. The lone dissenter was Jeannette Rankin of Montana, who had also voted against declaring war on Germany in World War I, and who on 11 December refused to vote when the United States declared war on Germany and Italy.

American Casualties

The Navy and Marine Corps had 2,086 officers and men killed or fatally wounded; 749 wounded men survived. The Army had 215 officers and men killed or fatally wounded, 360 others wounded who survived, and twenty-two missing. The Navy lost ninety-two aircraft, including five of those from the *Enterprise* which arrived in time to get mixed up in the fight, and had thirty-one more damaged. The Army lost ninety-six aircraft.

Rescue Operations

The *Oklahoma* and *Utah* capsized so quickly that some men were trapped below decks. Before the raid ended, men on nearby ships heard tapping coming from these two ships, and rescue efforts began at once. Cutting holes through the steel hull plates was a slow job. On the *Oklahoma,* the first six men were brought out the morning of 8 December. About noon eleven more were brought out; thirteen more were rescued during the day. The last man, number 32, was rescued early in the morning of 9 December. One man was rescued from the *Utah,* the rescue party hammering away to get him out while the raid was on.

Another tragedy of the Pearl Harbor affair was discovered in June of 1942 when the *West Virginia* was placed in dry dock for repairs. Records indicated that about seventy men had been trapped below decks and went down with the ship when she sank. The bodies of three men were found in a pump room where chalked messages on the wall showed that they had lived in their dark tomb until the day before Christmas eve, waiting for the rescue that never came.

The destroyer **Ward** ***began the war on Japan early Sunday morning when No. 3 gun crew sank a midget submarine outside Pearl Harbor. From left to right, the gunners were R. H. Knapp, C. W. Fenton, R. B. Nolde, A. A. Domagall, D. W. Gruening, J. A. Peick, H. P. Flanagan, E. J. Bukrey, and K. C. J. Lasch.***

The Tennessee, *relatively undamaged, looks down on the* West Virginia, *sitting on the bottom. Mainmast of the* Arizona *can be seen astern of the "WeeVee."*

Repair, Salvage, and Overhaul

The official report of damage to ships of the U.S. Fleet was as follows:

BATTLESHIPS *Arizona, California, West Virginia*—Sunk
Oklahoma—Capsized
Nevada—Heavily damaged
Maryland, Pennsylvania, Tennesssee—Damaged

LIGHT CRUISERS *Helena, Raleigh*—Heavily damaged
Honolulu—Damaged

DESTROYERS *Cassin, Shaw, Downes*—Heavily damaged

REPAIR SHIP *Vestal*—Badly damaged

MINELAYER *Oglala*—Sunk

SEAPLANE TENDER *Curtiss*—Damaged

AUXILIARY *Utah*—Capsized
Sotoyomo—Sunk

Salvage operations began on 14 December. Some of the jobs were fairly simple, although somewhat baffling—such as raising the floating dry dock in which the *Shaw* exploded. A perplexed sailor exclaimed, "How in hell can you sink a dry dock!" Divers went down and patched over 150 holes; then the dock was floated on 9 January and back in operation on 25 January, when the *Shaw* was again docked in it.

The *Shaw* had a false bow built on her, and sailed for the West Coast on 9 February. Rebuilt at Mare Island, she was back in the fleet by the end of 1942.

The *Cassin* and *Downes* were "scrapped" in the dry dock; their engines, shafts, and other machinery and usable equipment was removed and shipped back to Mare Island. There repair forces built new hulls around the engines. The Navy kept the names for the ships; the rebuilt *Cassin* won seven battle stars after she joined the fleet in February, 1944; the *Downes* was ready in November 1943 and won four battle stars.

The *Pennsylvania,* in dock with the *Cassin* and *Downes,* was taken out of dock on 12 December. She was repaired and left the Navy Yard on 20 December. The *Maryland* was also ready for service on 20 December. The *Honolulu* was ready for service on 12 January, 1942; the *Vestal* completed repairs on 18 February and the *Curtiss* on 28 May.

The *California* had to be patched up and pumped out before she could be raised. She was refloated on 24 March 1942, left Pearl Harbor on 10 October 1942 for the Puget Sound Navy Yard, where she was rebuilt and modernized. Part of the job involved installing 154 miles of new electrical cable. The *California* rejoined the fleet late in 1943 and won seven battle stars before the war ended.

Patching up the *West Virginia* required 650 tons of concrete. Some 800,000 gallons of fuel oil had to be pumped out of the ship before she could be raised on 17 May 1942. After temporary repairs, she sailed for the Puget Sound Navy Yard. She rejoined the fleet on 4 July 1944, won five battle stars, and sailed into Tokyo Bay for the Japanese surrender in 1945.

Salvage of the *Oklahoma* presented many problems. Not only had she sunk, she had rolled over, and righting a 35,000-ton ship was a terrifically complicated engineering problem. After 350,000 gallons of oil was pumped out, the ship was patched and filled with a huge air bubble which accounted for about 20,000 tons of her weight. Then twenty-one tall towers were fastened to the bottom of the ship, and three-inch cables ran from them to 20-ton electric winches on the shore. The ship was finally pulled right side up on 16 June 1943. She was refloated on 3 November, and dry docked on 28 December, where she was stripped of guns and machinery. The ship was decommissioned on 1 September 1944. Later she was sold for scrap, but in 1947 as two tugs towed her to the West Coast, she went down in a storm on 17 May.

The old *Oglala* was first considered a total loss, and plans were made to dynamite the wreck and raise the pieces for scrap, but this proved almost more difficult than raising the ship. She was finally floated on 23 April 1942, and given temporary repairs. Eventually she sailed to Mare Island on her own power, where she was rebuilt. She rejoined the fleet in February of 1944.

The *Utah,* built in 1909, was already obsolete, and raising her was estimated to cost perhaps $4,000,000, after which she would be worth only about $280,000 for scrap. The ship was never raised, but she has been declared a national cemetery. The *Arizona,* built in 1913, was so badly damaged there was no military value in the wreck, and it was determined that the ship should remain on the bottom, a memorial for the men who died in her.

In all the salvage operations, divers worked underwater for a total of about 20,000 hours without a single serious casualty, this despite the fact that the ships were loaded with fuel oil, ammunition, and in some cases, gasoline.

Despite having her bow blown off in dry dock, and having the dry dock sink under her, the* Shaw *was still afloat two days later. She was rebuilt and restored to duty.

Salvage of the* Oklahoma *involved slowly rolling her right side up again. Here she is on 19 March 1943, ninety degrees from the vertical position.

With all superstructure removed, the hulk of the* Oklahoma *entered drydock on 28 December 1943, more than two years after she went down.

The Pearl Harbor Investigations

In the years following Pearl Harbor, there were numerous investigations into every aspect of the affair, during which hundreds of people, American and Japanese, were interviewed and cross-examined. Briefly, they were:

The Roberts Commission convened on 18 December 1941, concluded on 23 January 1942. The record of proceedings and exhibits covered 2,173 printed pages.

The Hart Inquiry commenced on 12 February 1944 and concluded on 15 June 1944. The record of proceedings and exhibits ran to 565 printed pages.

The Army Pearl Harbor Board began its sessions on 20 July 1944 and concluded on 20 October 1944. The record covered 3,357 pages.

The Navy Court of Inquiry lasted from 24 July 1944 to 19 October 1944, and covered 1,397 pages.

The Clark Inquiry was conducted from 14 to 16 September 1944 and from 13 July to 4 August 1945. The record of proceedings covered 225 pages.

The Clausen Investigation commenced on 23 November 1944 and concluded on 12 September 1945. The report covered 695 pages.

The Hewitt Inquiry commenced on 14 May 1945 and concluded on 11 July 1945. The record covered 1,342 pages.

Joint Committee on the Investigation of the Pearl Harbor Attack. First hearings were held on 15 November 1945; the committee completed its work on 31 May 1946. The record covered 5,560 pages in 11 volumes. Pertinent exhibits and documents filled another 10 volumes. The additional exhibits and documents which were a part of all previous investigations mentioned above filled still another 9 volumes.

Unsung Heroes

Within minutes after the attack began, civilians as well as military men had reacted and were fighting fires, rescuing wounded, and digging trenches. Others served hot coffee, passed out lunches, helped in first aid stations, directed traffic, and donated blood. None of these people won medals and few were given commendations. If any among hundreds deserve special mention, it should be the Navy Yard's well-known photographer, Tai Sing Loo, who pitched in to fight fires, serve out food, and later wrote up his recollections of the day in one of the best pieces of literature to come out of the entire battle: *"How Happen I Were at Pearl Harbor."* He was on his way in to the yard to take a group photograph of the Marine guard when . . .

"Suddenly all excitement arouse the Honolulu Fire Engine rush down Bishop Street and all directions. Taxi full of sailor and marine dashing toward Pearl Harbor. I'm very much surprise what's all this excitement . . . I was great shock

Refloated, and with guns and mainmast removed, the* California *entered dry dock on 9 April 1942 for repairs. What appears to be a cage mast on seaplane tender* Curtis *(far left) is the Ford Island signal tower.

Tai Sing Loo, many years after Pearl Harbor, with his famous helmet. Admiral Nimitz once said that anyone who had not read Tai Sing Loo's account of the battle was not well informed on the attack on Pearl Harbor.

Wreckage of the midget submarine sunk in Pearl Harbor showing washboard effect of the depth charge attack by Monaghan.

The wreckage of a Japanese (Kate) aircraft hauled from the bottom of the harbor still clearly showed the red "meatball," and indications that it had probably burned before crashing.

with surprise the war are on. Watching many Japanee war planes . . . dropping bombs left and right . . . I wish my Graflex with me . . . second thought I change my mind . . . I didn't had my famous Trade-Mark helmet on . . . so I'm afraid some one will make a mistake me as a Jap and shot me down."

During the day Tai Sing Loo fought fires, directed traffic, and especially obtained and passed out food for dozens of tired and hungry men:

". . . I went to the garage to take my Red PutPut . . . some sandwiches ham and chicken, fruit all I can delivery . . . riding around and round the dry dock until every one had a sandwiches . . . I send 50 chicken and hams sandwiches apples and oranges and buns with ham to the shops supt. office. . . . At the Dry Dock all the workmen have no lunch and hungry, working on the USS Downs and USS Cassin, I ran short of everything about 6 pm. I told the men go to the Mess Hall . . . have their meal without charges and drink tomatoes juice and fruit. About 7:00 p.m. I went to the garage and have them take me to the Main gate. . . . My wife and four children were happy and thankful I were safely at home. As the Confucious say, 'Every Kind Deeds its return many, many time Folds.' "

Among the lesser-known heroes of the day were the half dozen sailors who comprised the crew of YG-17, a smelly little craft the Navy calls a "honey barge" Their usual job was to creep around the harbor, collecting garbage, but that day the YG-17, with no guns and only one fire hose, stayed alongside the *West Virginia* and fought fire until there was no more fire to fight.

Japanese Ships Assigned to "Hawaii Operation"

The action at Pearl Harbor on 7 December 1941 was a naval battle in which there was no direct contact with the enemy ships. Even the submarines which scouted Hawaii were undiscovered. All of the major ships in Japan's "Hawaii Operation" were sunk before the war ended.

TYPE	NAME	DATE AND PLACE SUNK BY U.S. NAVY	
CARRIER	*Akagi*	5 June 1942,	Battle of Midway
	Kaga	5 June 1942,	Battle of Midway
	Soryu	5 June 1942,	Battle of Midway
	Hiryu	5 June 1942,	Battle of Midway
	Shokaku	19 June 1944,	Battle of Philippine Sea
	Zuikaku	20 Oct. 1944,	Battle for Leyte Gulf
BATTLESHIPS	*Hiei*	13 Nov. 1942,	Battle for Guadalcanal
	Kirishima	15 Nov. 1942,	Battle for Guadalcanal
CRUISERS	*Tone*	28 July 1945,	Inland Sea of Japan
	Chikuma	25 Oct. 1944,	Battle for Leyte Gulf
	Katori	17 Feb. 1944,	Truk
	Abukuma	26 Oct. 1941,	Battle for Leyte Gulf
DESTROYERS	*Isokaze*	7 Apr. 1945,	East China Sea
	Tanikaze	9 June 1944,	Bonin Islands
	Hamakaze	7 Apr. 1945,	East China Sea
	Kasmui	7 Apr. 1945,	East China Sea
	Arare	5 July 1942,	Aleutian Islands
	Kagero	8 May 1943,	Solomon Islands
	Shiranuhi	27 Oct. 1944,	Luzon area, P.I.
	Akiguma	11 Apr. 1944,	Celebes Sea
	Urukaze	21 Nov. 1944,	Formosa
	Akebono	13 Nov. 1944,	Manila Bay
	Ushio		
	Sazanami	14 Jan. 1944,	Truk area
TANKERS	*Kyokuto Maru*	18 Sept. 1944,	South China Sea
	Kenyo Maru	14 Jan. 1944,	Palau area
	Kokuyo Maru	30 July 1944,	Sulu Sea
	Shikoku Maru	17 Feb. 1944,	Caroline Islands
	Akebono Maru	30 Mar. 1944,	Palau area
	Toho Maru	15 June 1945,	Gulf of Siam
	Nihon Maru		
	Toei Maru	18 Jan. 1943,	Rabaul area
SUBMARINES	*I-1*	29 Jan. 1943,	
	I-2	7 Apr. 1944,	New Ireland
	I-3	9 Dec. 1942,	Guadalcanal
	L-4	20 Dec. 1942,	New Britain
	I-5	19 July 1944,	Guam
	I-6	14 July 1944,	Marianas I.
	L-7	22 June 1943,	Aleutian I.
	I-8	31 Mar. 1945,	Okinawa
	I-9	10 May 1943,	Aleutian I.
	I-10	4 June 1944,	Marianas I.
	I-15	16 Dec. 1942,	Solomon I.
	I-16†	14 May 1944,	Solomon I.
	I-17	19 Aug. 1943,	Queensland, Aus.
	I-18†	2 Jan. 1943,	Solomon I.
	I-19	25 Nov. 1943,	Gilbert I.
	I-20†	1 Oct. 1943,	Solomon I.
	I-21	5 Feb. 1944,	Marshalls I.
	I-22†	12 Nov. 1942	New Georgia
	I-23	26 Feb. 1942,	
	I-24†	24 July 1943,	Admiralty I.
	I-68		
	I-69		
	I-71		
	I-72		
	I-73	27 Jan. 1942,	Midway
	I-74		
	I-75		

† Each of these submarines carried a midget 2-man submarine "piggyback" fashion. For details, see "Target A."

U.S. Fleet Disposition

Accounts of the Japanese attack on Pearl Harbor usually refer to "the fleet" being caught in the harbor, leading to the impression that the entire U.S. Pacific fleet was there. Actually, only half of the fleet was in Pearl Harbor—the rest was scattered all across the Pacific from Bremerton, Mare Island and San Diego on the West Coast to Wake, Midway, and Samoa.

All the Pacific Fleet battleships but one were in Pearl Harbor. There were no aircraft carriers in port at the time of the attack. Of other combatant types, there were in Pearl Harbor a total of eight cruisers, forty-one destroyers, and four submarines. Elsewhere that day, there were twelve cruisers, thirty-six destroyers, and eighteen submarines. In total numbers (including transports, tankers, and repair ships, but not miscellaneous yard craft) there were 106 ships in Pearl Harbor and 103 elsewhere. (See page 29, *Pacific Fleet Units in Pearl Harbor* and *Pacific Fleet Units at Sea or in West Coast Ports on 7 December 1941.*)

Task Force 8, consisting of *Enterprise, Northampton, Chester, Salt Lake City, Balch, Maury, Craven, Gridley, McCall, Dunlap, Fanning,* and *Ellet* was about 200 miles west of Oahu returning from Midway.

Task Force 12, consisting of *Lexington, Chicago, Portland, Astoria, Porter, Drayton, Flusser, Lamson* and *Mahan* was about 400 miles east of Midway, en route to that island.

Task Force 3, consisting of *Indianapolis, Hopkins, Southard, Dorsey, Elliot* and *Long* was operating off Johnston Island.

A group of ships carrying U.S. troops and cargo, Convoy No. 4002, and usually listed as the *Pensacola Convoy,* was westward bound near Samoa, en route to Manila. The *Pensacola* and *Niagara* were escorting the transports *Chaumont, Republic, Willard A. Holbrook, Meigs;* the U.S. merchant ships *Coast Farmer* and *Admiral Halstead;* and the Dutch ship *Bloemfontein.*

About thirty ships were at ports on the West Coast, another dozen were operating in the Hawaiian area, and another half dozen were at sea anywhere from Alaska to Peru.

Pacific Fleet Units in Pearl Harbor on 7 December 1941

(dates of loss indicated in brackets)

Allen DD66
Argonne AG31
Antares AKS3
Arizona BB39 [7 Dec. 1941]
Ash AN7
Avocet AVP4
Aylwin DD355
Bagley DD386
Blue DD387 [23 Aug. 1942]
Bobolink AM20
Breese DM18
Cachalot SS170
California BB44
Case DD370
Cassin DD372
Castor AKS1
Chew DD106
Cinchona YN7
Cockatoo AMc8
Condor AMc14
Conyngham DD371
Crossbill AMC9
Cummings DD365
Curtiss AV4
Dale DD353
Detroit CL8
Dewey DD349
Dobbin AD3
Dolphin SS169
Downes DD375
Farragut DD348
Gamble DM13
Grebe AM43 [5 Dec. 1942]
Helena CL50 [6 July 1943]
Helm DD388
Henley DD391 [3 Oct. 1943]
Honolulu CL48
Hull DD350 [18 Dec. 1944]
Hulbert AVD6
Jarvis DD393
Keosanqua AT38
MacDonough DD351
Maryland BB46
McFarland DD237
Medusa AR1
Monaghan DD354 [18 Dec. 1944]
Montgomery DM17
Mugford DD389
Narwhal SS167
Navajo AT64 [11 Sept. 1943]
Neosho AO23 [11 May 1942]
Nevada BB36
New Orleans CA32
Oglala CM4
Oklahoma BB37 [7 Dec. 1941]
Ontario AT13
Patterson DD392
Pelias AS14
Pennsylvania BB38
Perry DMS17 [13 Sept. 1944]
Phelps DD360
Phoenix CL46
Preble DM20
Pruitt DM22
Pyro AE1
Rail AM26
Raleigh CL7
Ralph Talbot DD390
Ramsey DM16
Reedbird AMc30
Reid DD369 [11 Dec. 1944]
Rigel AVD11
Sacramento PGS19
San Francisco CA38
Schley DD103
Selfridge DD357
Shaw DD373
Sicard DM21
Solace AH5
Sotoyomo
St. Louis CL49
Sumner AG32
Sunnadin AT28
Swan AVP7
Tangier AV8
Tautog SS199
Tennessee BB43
Tern AM31
Thornton AVD11
Tracy DM19
Trever DMS17
Tucker DD374 [4 Aug. 1942]
Turkey AM13
Utah AG4 [7 Dec. 1941]
Vestal AR4
Vireo AM52
Ward DD139 [7 Dec. 1944]
Wasmuth DMS15 [29 Dec. 1942]
West Virginia BB48
Whitney AD4
Widgeon ARS1
Worden DD352 [12 Jan. 1943]
Zane DMS14

YARDCRAFT

YC417
YDD68
YFD2
YG15
LG17
YO30
YO43
YR22
YT153
YNg17
YN53
YMT5
YN47
YTT3
YT129
YT146
YT119
YT130
YT152
YR20

Pacific Fleet Units at Sea or in West Coast Ports on 7 December 1941

(dates of loss indicated in brackets)

Aldebaran AF10 San Francisco
Arctic AF7 Lahaina Roads
Argonaut SM1 Midway [10 Jan. 1943]
Astoria CA34 TF12 [9 Aug. 1942]
Balch DD363 TF8
Ballard AVD10 transit SD-MI
Benham DD397 TF8 [15 Nov. 1942]
Boggs DMS3 off Oahu
Boreas AF9 San Francisco
Brazos AO4 off Dutch Harbor
Casco AVP12 PSNY
Chandler DMS9 off Oahu
Chester CA27 TF8
Chicago CA29 TF12 [30 Jan. 1943]
Clark DD361 NYMI
Colorado BB45 PSNY
Concord CL10 San Diego
Craven DD382 TF8
Cushing DD376 NYMI [13 Nov. 1942]
Cuttlefish SS171 NYMI
Cuyama AO3 San Diego
Dent DD116 San Diego
Dixie AD14 NYMI
Dorsey DMS1 TF3
Drayton DD366 TF12
Dunlap DD384 TF8
Ellet DD298 TF8
Elliot DMS4 TF3
Enterprise CV6 TF8
Fanning DD385 TF8
Flusser DD368 TF12
Fulton AS11 off Guatamala
Gar SS206 off Mexico
Gillis AVD12 Alaskan area
Harris AP8 San Diego
Hopkins DMS13 TF3
Hovey DMS11 off Oahu [6 Jan. 1945]
Indianapolis CA35 TF3 [30 July 1945]
Kanawha AO1 NYMI [7 Apr. 1943]
Kaskaskia AO27 NYMI
Kingfisher AM25 Samoa
Kuala AG33 Palmyra
Lamberton DMS2 off Oahu
Lamson DD367 TF12
Lexington CV2 TF12 [8 May 1942]
Litchfield DD336 off Oahu
Long DMS12 TF3 [6 Jan. 1945]
Louisville CA28 Solomon I. area
Mahan DD364 TF12 [7 Dec. 1944]
Maury DD401 TF8
McCall DD400 TF8
Minneapolis CA36 off Oahu
Nautilus SS168 NYMI
Neches AO5 enroute SF-PH [23 Jan. 1942]
Niagara Samoa area
Northampton CA26 TF8 [1 Dec. 1942]
Ortolan ASR5 San Diego
Pelican AV6 NYMI
Pensacola CA24 Samoa area
Perkins DD377 NYMI
Pinola AT33 San Pedro
Platte AO24 Los Angeles
Plunger SS179 enroute to Oahu
Pollack SS180 enroute to Oahu
Pompano SS181 enroute to Oahu [15 Oct. 1943]
Porter DD356 TF12
Portland CA33 TF12
Preston DD379 NYMI [14 Nov. 1942]
Procyon AK19 Alameda
Rathburne DD113 NYMI
Richmond CL9 off Peru
Robin AM3 off Oahu
Sabine AO25 NYMI
Salt Lake City CA25 TF8
Saratoga CV3 San Diego
Seagull AM30 Lahaina Roads
Sepulga AO20 near San Diego
Smith DD378 NYMI
Sonoma AT12 west of Oahu
Southard DMS10 TF3
S18 SS123 San Diego
S23 SS128 San Diego
S27 SS132 NYMI [19 June 1942]
S28 SS133 NYMI [4 June 1944]
S34 SS139 San Diego
S35 SS140 San Diego
Talbot DD114 San Diego
Tambor SS198 Wake Island
Teal AVP5 Seattle
Thresher SS200 off Oahu
Tippecanoe AO21 Wilmington, Cal.
Trenton CL11 Balboa, C.Z.
Triton SS201 Wake I. [10 Apr. 1943]
Trout SS202 Wake I. [17 Apr. 1944]
Tuna SS203 NYMI
Vega AK17 Honolulu
Waters DD115 San Diego
Williamson AVD2 PSNY
Wm. Ward Burrows AP6 en route Wake Island
Wright AV1 west of Oahu

ARIZONA MEMORIAL

Design Concept

"The form, wherein the structure sags in the center but stands strong and vigorous at the ends, expresses initial defeat and ultimate victory.

"Wide opening in walls and roof permit a flooding by sunlight and a close view of the sunken battleship eight feet below, both fore and aft. At low tide, as the sun shines upon the hull, the barnacles which encrust it shimmer like gold jewels . . . a beautiful sarcophagus.

"The overall effect is one of serenity. Overtones of sadness have been omitted to permit the individual to contemplate his own personal responses . . . his inner-most feelings."

Alfred Preis—ARCHITECT

By the time World War II ended, most of the wreckage in Pearl Harbor had been cleaned up. The one vivid reminder of the havoc of 7 December 1941 was the rusty ruin of the *Arizona,* and as new fighting ships joined the fleet they began the unofficial practice of rendering honors—saluting the wreck —as other ships had done before the war when the ship was in commission and flying her colors. Finally, on 7 March 1950, the Commander in Chief of the Pacific Fleet, Admiral Arthur Radford, made it official: "From today on the USS *Arizona* will again fly our country's flag. . . ." And from that day on, the U.S. flag has flown above the wreck of the *Arizona.*

By 1956 it was considered no longer safe to conduct the daily ceremony of colors aboard the ship, and the Commandant, Fourteenth Naval District invited the Pacific War Memorial Commission to sponsor a public campaign to obtain a memorial for the ship. Hawaii's Delegate to Congress, the Honorable John A. Burns, introduced legislation which the 85th Congress approved on 15 March 1958, authorizing construction of a memorial at Pearl Harbor.

Funds were raised in various ways. Congress appropriated $150,000, and the State of Hawaii contributed $100,000. A telecast of the "This is Your Life" show and a benefit performance by ex-GI Elvis Presley brought in $160,000. The AMVETS contributed the carillon, and paid for the Italian marble in the shrine.

The highly sensitive solution of the design problem by Architect Alfred Preis (see photograph, back cover) achieved a harmonious composition of space and light which must be experienced from within, rather than the customary pile of marble which can only be observed from without. The over-all design was handled by Johnson & Perkins, Preis Associates; the plans were turned into reality by the Walker-Moody Construction Company with the assistance of the Public Works Center at Pearl Harbor and various sub-contractors. Total cost was $532,000.

The structure is in the form of an enclosed bridge 184 feet long which is 36 feet wide and 21 feet high at the ends and tapers to 27 feet wide and 14 feet high at the center. It is supported by two 250-ton concrete girders which rest on 36 pre-stressed pilings driven into the harbor bottom; no part of the structure touches the hulk of the *Arizona.*

Within the memorial there are three sections: the museum room, containing mementos from the ship; the assembly room, which can accommodate 200 persons for ceremonies; and the shrine room, where on a wall are inscribed the names of 1,177 men who died when the ship went down. The oldest relic on display is the bell placed aboard the *Arizona* before she was commissioned on 17 October 1916.

Since the formal dedication of the memorial on 30 May 1962, millions of people, both from the United States and Japan, have visited there, arriving for various reasons and departing with various emotions. The visitors for whom the memorial has the deepest meaning still proudly call themselves *Arizona* sailors; they are the men who were there on 7 December 1941 and return to read the names of other *Arizona* sailors who are still there. For all the men in the *Arizona* on 7 December 1941, the memorial assures that the date

". . . shall ne'er go by,
From this day to the ending of the world,
But we in it shall be remembered, —
We few, we happy few, we band of brothers;
For he that today sheds his blood for me
Shall be my brother. . . ."

Battleships are considered to have a useful life of 20 years. The *Arizona,* laid down as World War I began in 1914, was technically obsolete long before World War II began in 1941. When war did come, her big guns never fired a shot, and she was on the bottom in a few short minutes. Yet the *Arizona* will be remembered for as long as any other of the Navy's famous fighting ships, for in those few short minutes her crew fought, as did all sailors, for ultimate victory.

Ships Named for Pearl Harbor Casualties

The Navy has long had a tradition of naming some of its fighting ships for some of its fighting men. This custom, continued during World War II, gave the Navy a whole fleet of ships honoring heroes in all ranks from seaman to admiral. The war was short for the following named men; most of them died in the first hour, but their names were carried proudly by destroyers, destroyer escorts and destroyers transports which fought their way back across the Pacific to Japan.

Here follows a list of seventy-five ships named for men who died at Pearl Harbor, with type designation and hull number, name and rank of the man for which named, and the ship or duty station in which he served on 7 December 1941, if known.

Austin DE15 John A. Austin, Chief Carpenter's Mate, *Oklahoma*

Barber APD57 Malcolm J. Barber, Leroy K. Barber, and Randolph H. Barber, all Firemen, *Oklahoma*

Bates APD47 Edward M. Bates, Ensign, *Arizona*

Bennion DD662 Mervyn S. Bennion, Captain, *West Virginia*

Booth DE170 Robert S. Booth, Jr., Ensign, *Arizona*

Bowers APD40 Robert K. Bowers, Ensign, *California*

Buckley DE51 John D. Buckley, Aviation Ordnanceman, NAS Kaneohe Bay

Charles Lawrence APD37 Charles Lawrence, Aviation Machinist's Mate, NAS Kaneohe Bay

Christopher DE100 Harold J. Christopher, Ensign, *Nevada*

Connolly DE306 John G. Connolly, Chief Pay Clerk, *Oklahoma*

Crowley DE303 Thomas E. Crowley, Lieutenant Commander, *Arizona*

Darby DE218 Marshall E. Darby, Ensign

Day DE225 Francis D. Day, Chief Watertender, *Oklahoma*

Daniel T. Griffin APD38 Aviation Machinist's Mate, NAS Kaneohe Bay

Edward C. Daly DE17 Edward C. Daly, Coxswain, ...

Emery DE28 Jack M. Emery, Ensign, ...

England APD41 John C. England, Ensign, *Oklahoma*

Finnegan DE307 William M. Finnegan, Ensign, *Oklahoma*

Flaherty DE135 Francis C. Flaherty, Ensign, *Oklahoma*

Formoe DE509 Clarence M. Formoe, Aviation Machinist's Mate, NAS Kaneohe Bay

Foss DE59 Rodney S. Foss, Ensign, Patrol Squadron 11

Frederick C. Davis DE136 Frederick C. Davis, Ensign, *Nevada*

Gantner APD42 Samuel M. Gantner, Boatswain's Mate, *Nevada*

George W. Ingram APD43 George W. Ingram, Seaman, ...

Gosselin APD126 Edward W. Gosselin, Ensign, *Arizona*

Halloran DE305 William I. Halloran, Ensign, *Arizona*

Harveson DE316 Harold Aloysius Harveson, Lt(jg), *Utah*

Haverfield DE393 James W. Haverfield, Ensign, *Arizona*

Herbert C. Jones DE137 Herbert C. Jones, Ensign, *California*

Hill DE141 Edwin J. Hill, Chief Boatswain, *Nevada*

Hollis APD86 Ralph Hollis, Ensign, *Arizona*

Howard D. Crow DE252 Howard D. Crow, Ensign, *Maryland*

Ira Jeffery APD44 Ira W. Jeffery, Ensign,

James E. Craig DE201 James E. Craig, LCDR, *Pennsylvania*

Jordan DE204 Julian B. Jordan, Lt., *Oklahoma*

J. Richard Ward DE243 James R. Ward, Seaman, *Oklahoma*

Kidd DD661 Isaac C. Kidd, Rear Admiral, *Arizona*

Kirkpatrick DE318 Thomas L. Kirkpatrick, Captain (ChC), *Arizona*

Lake DE301 John E. Lake, Jr., Acting Pay Clerk, *Arizona*

Lamons DE743 Kenneth T. Lamons, Boatswain's Mate, *Nevada*

Leopold DE319 Robert L. Leopold, Ensign, *Arizona*

Manlove DE36 Arthur C. Manlove, Electrician, *Arizona*

Manning DE199 Milburn A. Manning, Aviation Machinist's Mate, NAS Kaneohe Bay

Marsh DE699 Benjamin R. Marsh, Jr., Ensign, *Arizona*

McClelland DE750 Thomas A. McClelland, Ensign, ...

Menges DE320 Herbert H. Menges, Ensign, Fighting Squadron 6, *Enterprise*

Merrill DE392 Howard D. Merrill, Ensign

Moore DE240 Fred K. Moore, Seaman, *Arizona*

Neundorf DE200 William F. Neundorf, Seaman, *Nevada*

Newman APD59 Laxton G. Newman, Aviation Machinist's Mate, NAS Kaneohe Bay

O'Neill DE188 William T. O'Neill, Ensign, *Arizona*

Otterstetter DE244 Carl W. Otterstetter, Seaman, NAS Kaneohe Bay

Pride DE323 Lewis B. Pride, Jr., Ensign, *Oklahoma*

Rall DE304 Richard R. Rall, Lt(jg), ...

Reeves APD52 Thomas J. Reeves, Chief Radioman, ...

Register APD92 Paul J. Register, LCDR, *Arizona*

Richey DE385 Joseph L. Richey, Ensign, Observation Squadron 2

Sanders DE40 Eugene T. Sanders, Chief Boatswain, ...

Schmitt APD76 Aloysius H. Schmitt, Lt(jg), *Oklahoma*

Scott DE214 Robert R. Scott, Machinist's Mate, *California*

Sederstrom DE31 Delmore Sederstrom, Ensign, *Oklahoma*

Smartt DE257 Joseph G. Smartt, Ensign, NAS Kaneohe Bay

Solar DE221 Adolfor Solar, Boatswain's Mate, *Nevada*

Stern DE187 Charles M. Stern, Jr., Ensign, *Oklahoma*

Stockdale DE399 Lewis S. Stockdale, Ensign, *Oklahoma*

Thomas J. Gary DE326 Thomas J. Gary, Seaman, *California*

Tills DE748 Robert G. Tills, Ensign, ...

Tomich DE242 Peter Tomich, Chief Watertender, *Utah*

Uhlmann DD687 Robert W. Uhlmann, Ensign, NAS Kaneohe Bay

Van Valkenburgh DD656 Franklin Van Valkenburgh, Captain, *Arizona*

Walter S. Brown DE258 Walter S. Brown, Aviation Machinists's Mate, NAS Kaneohe Bay

Weaver DE741 Luther D. Weaver, Seaman, NAS Kaneohe Bay

William C. Miller DE259 William C. Miller, Radioman, ...

Willis DE395 Walter M. Willis, Ensign, Scouting Squadron Six, *Enterprise*

Wyman DE38 Eldon P. Wyman, Ensign, *Oklahoma*

MEDAL OF HONOR

Bennion, Mervyn, Captain, USN

Finn, John W., Lt(jg), USN

Flaherty, Francis C., Ensign, USN

Fuqua, Samuel G., Captain, USN

Hill, Edwin J., Chief Boatswain, USN

Jones, Herbert C., Ensign, USNR

Kidd, Isaac C., Rear Admiral, USN

Reeves, Thomas J., Chief Radioman, USN

Ross, Donald K., Lt., USN

Scott, Robert R., Machinist's mate first class, USN

Tomich, Peter, Chief Watertender, USN

Van Valkenburgh, Franklin, Captain, USN

Ward, James Richard, Seaman first class, USN

Young, Cassin, Captain, USN

NAVY CROSS

Baker, Lionel H., Pharmacist's Mate second class, USN
Bolser, Gordon E., Lt(jg), USN
Bothne, Adolph M., Boatswain, USN
Burford, William P., LCDR, USN
Christopher, Harald J., Ensign, USNR
Curtis, Ned B., Pharmacist's Mate second class, USN
Daly, Edward Carlyle, Coxswain, USN
Darling, Willard D., Corporal, USMC
Davis, Frederick C., Ensign, USNR
Dickinson, Clarence E., Jr., Lieutenant, USN
Douglas, C. E., Gunnery Sgt., USMC
Driskell, J. R., Corporal, USMC
Dunlap, Ernest H., Jr., Ensign, USN
Edwards, John Perry, Ensign, USNR
Etchell, George D., Chief Shipfitter, USN
Fenno, Frank W., Lt., USN
Fisler, Frank M., Ensign, USNR
Fleming, W. D., Boatswain's Mate first class, USN
Bombasy, L. G., Seaman second class, USN
Graham, Donald A., Aviation Machinist's Mate first class, USN
Hailey, Thomas E., Sgt., USMC
Hansen, Alfred L., Chief Machinist's Mate, USN
Huttenberg, Allen J., Ensign, USNR
Isquith, Solomon S., LCDR, USN
Jewell, Jesse D., Cdr(MC), USN
Kauffman, Draper L., Lt., USNR
Larson, Nils R., Ensign, USN
Ley, F. C., Jr., Fireman second class, USNR
McMurtry, Paul J., Boatswain's Mate first class, USN
Mead, Harry R., Radioman second class, USN
Miller, Doris, Mess attendant first class, USN
Miller, Jim D., Lt(jg), USN
Moore, Fred K., Seaman first class, USN
Outerbridge, William W., LCDR, USN
Parker, William W., Seaman first class, USN
Peterson, Robert J., Radioman second class, USN
Pharris, Jackson C., Gunner, USN
Phillips, John S., Cdr., USN
Riggs, Cecil D., LCDR(MC), USN
Robb, James W., Jr., Lt(jg), USN
Roberts, William R., Radioman second class, USN
Ruth, Wesley H., Ensign, USN
Singleton, Arnold, Ensign, USNR
Smith, Harold F., Boatswain's Mate second class, USN
Snyder, J. L., Yeoman first class, USN
Taussig, Joseph K., Jr., Ensign, USN
Taylor, Thomas H., Ensign, USN
Teaff, Perry L., Ensign, USN
Thatcher, Albert C., Aviation Machinist's Mate second class, USN
Thomas, Francis J., LCDR, USN
Thomas, Robert E., Jr., Ensign, USN
Vaeesen, John B., Fireman second class, USNR

SILVER STAR MEDAL

Kiefer, Edwin H., Lt(jg), USNR

Marshall, Theodore W., Lt., USNR

Owen, George T., Commodore, USN

Shapley, Alan, Major, USMC

NAVY AND MARINE CORPS MEDAL

Day, Francis D., Chief Watertender, USN

Schmitt, Aloysius H., Lt(jg) ChC., USN

Thomas, William S., Shipfitter first class, USN

Wright, Paul R., Chief Watertender, USNR

Army Awards for Heroism included five Distinguished Service Crosses and sixty-five Silver Stars.